PENGUIN LIFE

SIX THINKING HATS

Edward de Bono invented the concept of lateral thinking. A world-renowned writer and philosopher, he is the leading authority in the field of creative thinking and the direct teaching of thinking as a skill. In the decades since Dr de Bono introduced lateral thinking, the concept has become so entrenched in our language that it is used equally in physics lectures, television comedies or brainstorming sessions. His key contribution has been his understanding of the brain as self-organising system. His work spans generations, continents and belief systems, and is equally influential in the boardrooms of leading businesses such as Apple and British Airways as on the shelves of classrooms in rural Africa.

Dr de Bono has written more than sixty books, in forty languages, with people now teaching his methods worldwide. He has chaired a special summit of Nobel Prize laureates, had faculty appointments at the universities of Oxford, London, Cambridge and Harvard, and been hailed as one of the 250 people who have contributed most to mankind.

Dr de Bono's classic bestsellers include *Six Thinking Hats*, *Lateral Thinking*, *I Am Right You Are Wrong*, *How To Be More Interesting*, *Teach Yourself To Think*, *Teach Your Child How To Think*, and *Simplicity*.

www.debono.com

Six Thinking Hats®

Edward de Bono

Revised and Updated

PENGUIN LIFE

AN IMPRINT OF

PENGUIN BOOKS

PENGUIN LIFE

UK | USA | Canada | Ireland | Australia
India | New Zealand | South Africa

Penguin Life is part of the Penguin Random House group of companies whose addresses can be found at global.penguinrandomhouse.com.

First published in the United States of America by Little, Brown and Company 1985
Revised and updated edition published by First Back Bay 1999
Published in Great Britain by Penguin Books 2000
008

For more information about training in Dr de Bono's methods, see www.debono.com

Printed in Great Britain by Clays Ltd, Elcograf S.p.A

A CIP catalogue record for this book is available from the British Library

ISBN: 978–0–241–25753–1

www.greenpenguin.co.uk

Contents

Preface

The Six Thinking Hats method may well be the most important change in human thinking for the past twenty-three hundred years.

That may seem a rather exaggerated claim but the evidence is beginning to point that way. When this book was first published fourteen years ago, such a claim would have been nonsense. But over the years, the evidence to support it has been steadily accumulating.

A major corporation (ABB) used to spend thirty days on their multinational project team discussions. Using the parallel thinking of the Six Hats method, the discussions now take as little as two days. A researcher from a top IBM laboratory told me that the Six Hats method had reduced meeting times to one quarter of what they had been. Statoil in Norway had a problem with an oil rig that was costing about one hundred thousand dollars a day. A certified trainer, Jens Arup, introduced the Six Hats method and in twelve minutes the problem was solved – and the one-hundred-thousand-dollar-a-day expenditure was reduced to nil. There were two similar law cases: in one case the jury took more than three hours to reach a decision. In the second case, one juror introduced the Six Hats method. A decision was reached in fifteen minutes. In a simple experiment with three hundred senior civil servants, the introduction of the Six Hats method increased thinking productivity by 493 per cent.

Those examples show huge changes. We are normally

very happy with productivity increases of 5 or 10 per cent. Here we have changes of 500 per cent and more. Something is happening.

Widespread Use Around the World

I can report that the Six Hats method is now very widely used around the world. When I first designed the concept I had no idea how rapid the spread would be. The method is simple, robust and effective – which accounts for the very widespread use.

Last year I received two letters on the same day. One letter was from the head of research at Siemens in Germany. Siemens is by far the largest corporation in Europe with close to four hundred thousand employees and a turnover in excess of sixty billion dollars. They now have thirty-seven internal trainers in my methods and every department has a special 'innovation unit' based on my methods. In his letter, the head of research told how he had used the Six Hats method with success at a senior research meeting. The second letter was from Simon Batchelor, who had been on an aid mission to Cambodia to help the Khmer villagers drill for water. He found it difficult to get the villagers involved in the process. He had my book *Teach Your Child How to Think* with him and, from this book, he taught the Six Hats method to the Khmer villagers. They became so enthusiastic that they told him that learning to think was more important than drilling for water.

A few days later I was in Wellington, New Zealand, and the head teacher of Wellesley School (a leading school in New Zealand) told me that he was teaching the method to five-year-olds. (A few months later, the head teacher of Clayfield College in Brisbane told me that they even taught it to four-year-olds.) A week after being in New Zealand I spoke at a major Microsoft marketing meeting in Seattle and introduced the attendees to the parallel thinking of the Six Hats method. The method has been used by NASA, IBM, DuPont, NTT (Japan), Shell, BP, Statoil (Norway), Marzotto (Italy), and Federal Express, among many others. This shows the remarkable adaptability of the Six Hats method: it can be taught with equal success to top-level executives and to pre-school children.

The Six Hats Method

Thinking is the ultimate human resource. Yet we can never be satisfied with our most important skill. No matter how good we become, we should always want to be better. Usually, the only people who are very satisfied with their thinking skill are those poor thinkers who believe that the purpose of thinking is to prove yourself right – to your own satisfaction. If we have only a limited view of what thinking can do, we may be smug about our excellence in this area, but not otherwise.

The main difficulty of thinking is confusion. We try to do too much at once. Emotions, information, logic, hope and creativity all crowd in on us. It is like juggling with too many balls.

What I am putting forward in this book is a very simple concept which allows a thinker to do one thing at a time. He or she becomes able to separate emotion from logic, creativity from information, and so on. The concept is that of the six thinking hats. Putting on any one of these hats defines a certain type of thinking. In the book I describe the nature and contribution of each type of thinking.

The six thinking hats allow us to conduct our thinking as a conductor might lead an orchestra. We can call forth what we will. Similarly, in any meeting it is very useful to switch people out of their usual track in order to get them to think differently about the matter in hand.

It is the sheer *convenience* of the six thinking hats that is the main value of the concept.

Special Note on the Black Hat

I am writing this special note because a few people have misinterpreted the black hat and have somehow regarded it as a bad hat. On the contrary, the black hat is the most valuable of all the hats and certainly the most used. Using the black hat means being careful and cautious. The black hat points out difficulties, dangers and potential problems. With the black hat you avoid danger to yourself, to others and to the community. It is under the black hat that you point out possible dangers.

For the most part, the thrust of Western thinking has been the 'black hat' with an emphasis on critical thinking and caution. It prevents mistakes, excesses and nonsenses.

Notes on the New Edition

Today, there is a huge amount of experience using the Six Hats method. This was not the case when I first wrote the book. The method can therefore be introduced with confidence. It is no longer a matter of trying out something new and exotic. It is now a matter of catching up with a powerful thinking method that has been in use for fourteen years across all ages, cultures and abilities.

People are sometimes hesitant about the hats and colours because they do not seem serious or complicated enough (some people love complexity). In practice, the simplicity has never been a problem. People realize they need the hats and colours as simple mental hooks. Hats and colours are much easier to remember than are complicated psychological terms.

This revised and updated edition is based on my experience using and working with the Six Hats method. Over the years it has become apparent that the method is both powerful and easy to use. The effectiveness of the method is much greater than I had ever imagined. It is an alternative to the argument system, which was never intended to be constructive or creative. With the Six Hats method the emphasis is on 'what can be' rather than just on 'what is', and on how we design a way forward – not on who is right and who is wrong.

Chapter 1

Introduction

An antelope grazing in Africa hears a sound in the grass. Immediately all the neuronal clusters concerned with danger are activated so that the lion is recognized as soon as it emerges from the grass, and the antelope is able to escape. Such sensitization is a key part of how the brain works and why it is so efficient.

It is not possible to be sensitized in different directions at the same time just as it would not be possible to design a golf club that was the best club for driving and at the same time the best club for putting. That is why the Six Hats method is essential. It allows the brain to maximize its sensitivity in different directions at different times. It is simply not possible to have that maximum sensitization in different directions all at the same time.

Argument versus Parallel Thinking

The basic idea behind Western thinking was designed about twenty-three hundred years ago by the Greek 'Gang of Three' and is based on argument.

Socrates put great emphasis on dialectic and argument. In 80 per cent of the dialogues in which he was involved (as written down by Plato) there is no constructive outcome at all. Socrates saw his role as simply pointing out what was 'wrong'. He wanted to clarify the correct use of concepts like justice and love by pointing out incorrect usage. Plato believed that the 'ultimate' truth was hidden below appearances. His famous analogy is of a person chained up in a cave so that he can see only the back wall of the cave. There is a fire at the entrance to the cave. After a person enters the cave, his shadow is projected on to the back wall of the cave and that is all the chained-up person can see. Plato used this analogy to point out that as we go through life we can see only the 'shadows' of the truth.

Aristotle systematized inclusion/exclusion logic. From past experience we would put together 'boxes', definitions, categories or principles. When we came across something, we judged into which box it fell. Something could be in the box or not in the box. It could not be half in and half out – nor could it be anywhere else.

As a result, Western thinking is concerned with 'what is', which is determined by analysis, judgement and argument.

That is a fine and useful system. But there is another whole aspect of thinking that is concerned with 'what can be', which involves constructive thinking, creative thinking and 'designing a way forward'.

In 1998, I was asked to give an opening talk at the Australian Constitutional Convention that was looking at the future of federation. I told the following story.

Once upon a time a man painted half his car white and the other half black. His friends asked him why he did such a strange thing. He replied: 'Because it is such fun, whenever I have an accident, to hear the witnesses in court contradict each other.'

At the end of the convention the chairperson, Sir Anthony Mason, told me that he was going to use that story because it is so often the case in an argument that both sides are right but are looking at different aspects of the situation.

Many cultures in the world, perhaps even the majority of cultures, regard argument as aggressive, personal and non-constructive. That is why so many cultures readily take up the parallel thinking of the Six Hats method.

A Changing World

A thinking system based on argument is excellent just as the front left wheel of a car is excellent. There is nothing wrong with it at all. But it is not sufficient.

A doctor is treating a child with a rash. The doctor immediately thinks of some possible 'boxes'. Is it sunburn? Is it food allergy? Is it measles? The doctor then examines the signs and symptoms and makes a judgement. If the doctor judges that the condition fits into the 'measles' box, then the treatment of measles is written on the side of that 'box' and the doctor knows exactly what to do. That is traditional thinking at its best.

From the past we create standard situations. We judge into which 'standard situation box' a new situation falls. Once we have made this judgement, our course of action is clear.

Such a system works very well in a stable world. In a stable world the standard situations of the past still apply. But in a changing world the standard situations may no longer apply.

Instead of judging our way forward, we need to design our way forward. We need to be thinking about 'what can be', not just about 'what is'.

Yet the basic tradition of Western thinking (or any other thinking) has not provided a simple model of constructive thinking. That is precisely what the Six Hats method (parallel thinking) is all about.

What Is Parallel Thinking?

There is a large and beautiful country house. One person is standing in front of the house. One person is standing behind the house. Two other people are standing at each side of the house. All four have a different view of the house. All four are arguing (by intercom) that the view each is seeing is the correct view of the house.

Using parallel thinking they all walk around and look at the front. Then they all walk around to the side, then the back and finally the remaining side. So at each moment each person is looking in parallel from the same point of view.

This is almost the exact opposite of argument, adversarial, confrontational thinking where each party deliberately takes an opposite view. Because each person eventually looks at all sides of the building, the subject is explored fully. Parallel thinking means that at any moment everyone is looking in the same direction.

But parallel thinking goes even further. In traditional thinking, if two people disagree, there is an argument in which each tries to prove the other party wrong. In parallel thinking, both views, no matter how contradictory, are put down in parallel. If, later on, it is essential to choose between the different positions, then an attempt to choose is made at that point. If a choice cannot be made, then the design has to cover both possibilities.

At all times the emphasis is on designing a way forward.

Directions and Hats

The essence of parallel thinking is that at any moment everyone is looking in the same direction – but the direction can be changed. An explorer might be asked to look north or to look east. Those are standard direction labels. So we need some direction labels for thinking. What are the different directions in which thinkers can be invited to look?

This is where the hats come in.

In many cultures there is already a strong association between thinking and 'thinking hats' or 'thinking caps'. The value of a hat as a symbol is that it indicates a role. People are said to be wearing a certain hat. Another advantage is that a hat can be put on or taken off with ease. A hat is also visible to everyone around. For those reasons I chose hats as the symbols for the directions of thinking.

Although physical hats are sometimes used, the hats are usually imaginary. Posters of the hats on the walls of meeting rooms often are used, however, as a reminder of the directions. There are six coloured hats corresponding to the six directions of thinking: white, red, black, yellow, green, blue.

Directions Not Descriptions

It is very important to note that the hats are directions and not descriptions of what has happened. It is not a matter of everyone saying what they like and then the hats being used to describe what has been said. It is a matter of setting out to think in that direction.

'Let's have some white hat thinking here' means a deliberate focus on information. Everyone now tries to think of information that is available, information that is needed, questions to be asked, other ways of getting information, and so on.

'I want your red hat on this' is a specific request for feelings, intuition and emotions on a particular issue.

'That is good black hat thinking; now let us switch to some yellow hat thinking . . .' In this case the term *black hat* describes thinking that seems to be cautious and seems to point out possible difficulties, but the main intention is to ask for a switch to the yellow hat direction (benefits, values, and so forth).

It is extremely important to appreciate the difference between description and direction. A description is concerned with what has happened. A direction is concerned with what is about to happen.

'I want you to look to the east' is very different from 'You have been looking to the east.'

'I want you to cook some scrambled eggs' is very different from 'I see that you have cooked some scrambled eggs.'

Not Categories of People

It is possible to create tests to determine whether a person is type A or type B, or any similar descriptive discriminations. Psychologists do that all the time. The difficulty is that once people have been put into 'boxes' they tend to stay there. Again, that is an example of 'what is' instead of 'what can be'.

In a race a thin man would usually beat a fat man ('what is'). But if the fat man learns to ride a bicycle, then the fat man will beat the thin man ('what can be').

There is a huge temptation to use the hats to describe and categorize people, such as 'she is black hat' or 'he is a green-hat person'. That temptation must be resisted. The hats are not descriptions of people but modes of behaviour.

It is true that some people may be permanently cautious and inclined to look for dangers. It is true that some people might always be bubbling with ideas and others might be better at focusing on facts. People may prefer one mode to another. People might be better at one mode than another. Nevertheless, the hats are not categories of people.

If you drive a car with manual gears, you use all the gears. In the engine of your car all the cylinders are firing. The hats are directions of thinking. Every person must be able, and skilled, to look in all the directions.

For those reasons the use of the hats as labels is dangerous because it destroys the whole point of the system, which is that everyone can look in every direction.

Note on Using the Thinking Hats

When people tell me that they have been using the Six Hats method, I often ask how they have been using it, and discover that sometimes they have been using it incorrectly. In a meeting, someone has been chosen as the black hat thinker, someone else as the white hat thinker, and so on. The people then keep those roles for the whole meeting. That is almost exactly the opposite of how the system should be used. The whole point of parallel thinking is that the experience and intelligence of everyone should be used in each direction. So everyone present wears the black hat at the appointed time. Everyone present wears the white hat at another time. That is parallel thinking and makes fullest use of everyone's intelligence and experience.

Showing Off

Many people tell me that they enjoy argument because they can show off how clever they are. They can win arguments and demolish opponents. None of that is very constructive but there may be a human need to show off.

Thus showing off is not excluded from parallel thinking and the Six Hats method. A thinker now shows off by showing how many considerations he or she can put forward under the yellow hat, how many under the black hat, and so forth. You show off by performing well as a thinker. You show off by performing better as a thinker than others in the meeting. The difference is that this type of showing off is constructive. The ego is no longer tied to being right.

Playing the Game

There are all sorts of attempts made to change the personalities of people. It is believed that if you point out a personality type or a weakness, the person will seek to compensate for that weakness. Such methods are generally slow, ineffective and do not work.

Once people are put into a certain 'box' or category they may try to compensate. But the effort of compensation reminds them of 'what they are', so they sink even deeper into that category.

Ever since Freud, the emphasis has been on analysis: find out the deep truths and motivations for action. Confucius's approach was almost the exact opposite. Instead of focusing on personality he chose to focus directly on behaviour. He urged you to use the right behaviour with your colleagues, your subordinates, your superiors and your family. Confucius was not the least bit interested in your personality or psychological make-up.

The Six Hats method follows the Confucian approach rather than the analytical one. The rules of behaviour are laid out. You follow those rules. If you are aggressive, no one is going to try to make you less aggressive. But if the yellow hat is in use, then you are to use your aggression in that direction.

By going straight to behaviour, the Six Hats method is much more acceptable and effective and quick than methods that set out to change personalities.

The 'game' aspect of the Six Hats is very important. If a game is being played, then anyone who does not obey the rules of the game is considered uncooperative. If there is a switch from the black hat (caution) to the yellow hat (possible benefits) and a person continues to lay out the potential dangers, then that person is seen to be refusing to play the game. Getting people to 'play the game' is a very powerful form of changing behaviour.

Results

Over the years the results of using the Six Hats method have become increasingly clear. The results are based on feedback from many sources and fall into four broad categories that are summarized here.

Power

With the Six Hats method, the intelligence, experience and knowledge of all the members of the group are fully used. Everyone is looking and working in the same direction.

A magnet is powerful because all the particles are aligned in the same direction. That is not the case with argument or free discussion. With the argument mode (as in a court of law), each party seeks to win the case. If one party thinks of a point that might benefit the other party, then that point is never raised. The purpose is to win, not to explore the subject honestly.

It is totally absurd that a person should hold back information or a point of view because revealing it would weaken his or her argument. The focusing of the sun's rays can melt the toughest of metals. In the same way, the focusing of the mental ability of many people on a problem can more easily solve that problem.

Time Saving

Optus (in Australia) had set aside four hours for an important discussion. Using the Six Hats method the discussion was concluded in forty-five minutes.

From every side there are reports of how much quicker meetings become when the six hats are used. Meetings take half the time. Meetings take a third or a quarter of the time. Sometimes, as in the case of ABB, meetings take one-fifteenth of the time.

In the United States, managers spend nearly 40 per cent of their time in meetings. If the Six Hats method reduced all meeting times by 75 per cent, you would have created 30 per cent more manager time – at no extra cost whatsoever.

In normal thinking or argument, if someone says something, then others have to respond – even if only out of politeness. But that is not the case with parallel thinking.

With parallel thinking, every thinker at every moment is looking in the same direction. The thoughts are laid out in parallel. You do not respond to what the last person has said. You simply add another idea in parallel. In the end, the subject is fully explored quickly.

Normally, if two points of view are at odds, then they are argued out. With parallel thinking, both points of view are laid out alongside each other. Later on, if it is essential to decide between the two, a decision is made. So there is not argument at every step.

Removal of Ego

Perhaps the biggest obstacle to quick and effective thinking is the ego. People tend to use thinking to parade their egos.

Thinking is used to attack and put down other people. Thinking is used to get your own way. Thinking is used to show others how clever you are. Thinking is used to express personal antagonisms.

Someone will choose to disagree on a point simply to show up the person who has made that point. If another person had made the point, there would have been full agreement. In general, we do not fully realize just how obstructive the ego is in preventing effective thinking.

During jury deliberations, there are often two personalities who refuse to agree whatever the evidence might be. Judges have told me that there is a much more serious problem than most people realize. Clearly, the problem destroys the basic value of the jury system. That is why there is now interest in several countries in training all juries in the Six Hats method. This would speed up deliberations by removing the ego problem.

Confrontational and adversarial thinking exacerbate the ego problem. Six Hats thinking removes it. With the Six Hats method you exert your ego by performing well as a thinker under each of the hats.

The Six Hats method provides neutral and objective exploration of a subject – argument does not.

One Thing at a Time

Confusion is the biggest enemy of good thinking. We try to do too many things at the same time. We look for information. We are affected by feelings. We seek new ideas and options. We have to be cautious. We want to find benefits. Those are a lot of things that need doing.

Juggling with six balls at the same time is rather difficult. Tossing up one ball at a time is much easier.

With the Six Hats method, we try to do only one thing at a time. There is a time when we look for danger (black hat). There is a time when we seek new ideas (green hat). There is a time when we focus on information (white hat). We do not try to do everything at the same time.

With colour printing, each colour is printed separately, one at a time, and in the end the full colour effect is obtained. It is the same with Six Hat thinking – we do one thing at a time and in the end the full picture emerges.

Underneath all this is the absolute physiological need to separate out the types of thinking. As I mentioned in the introduction, the brain is sensitized to look for danger and sensitized to seek benefits through a different chemical setting.

Aeroplanes coming in to land often fly over car parks. If you tell yourself to notice the yellow cars, then suddenly the yellow cars stand out and make themselves visible. That is an example of sensitization.

You cannot be sensitized in different directions at the same time, so when we set out to do all aspects of thinking in the same moment, we are going to be suboptimal on all of them.

All the points mentioned in this section may seem obvious and logical. In fact, there is no mystery about them. When the Six Hats method is used, the advantages soon become clear. Instead of rambling, ego-driven meetings, meetings are now constructive, productive and much faster.

People do not choose argument because it is the preferred method. They simply do not know any other way. The Six Hats provides another way.

Chapter 2

Six Hats, Six Colours

Each of the six thinking hats has a colour: white, red, black, yellow, green, blue. The colour provides the name for the hat.

I could have chosen clever Greek names to indicate the type of thinking required by each hat. That would have been impressive and would have pleased some people. But it would be of little practical value since the names would be difficult to remember.

I want thinkers to *visualize* and to imagine the hats as actual hats. For this to happen colour is important. How else could you distinguish between the hats? Different shapes would again be difficult to learn and would be confusing. Colour makes the imaging easier.

The colour of each hat is also related to its function.

White Hat White is neutral and objective. The white hat is concerned with objective facts and figures.

Red Hat Red suggests anger (seeing red), rage and emotions. The red hat gives the emotional view.

Black Hat Black is sombre and serious. The black hat is cautious and careful. It points out the weaknesses in an idea.

Yellow Hat Yellow is sunny and positive. The yellow hat is optimistic and covers hope and positive thinking.

Green Hat Green is grass, vegetation and abundant, fertile growth. The green hat indicates creativity and new ideas.

Blue Hat Blue is cool, and it is also the colour of the sky, which is above everything else. The blue hat is concerned with control, the organization of the thinking process and the use of the other hats.

If you remember the colour and the associations of each hat, remembering the function of the hat will then follow. You may also think of three pairs of hats:

White and red
Black and yellow
Green and blue

In practice the hats are *always* referred to by their colour and *never* by their function. There is a good reason for this. If you ask someone to give his or her emotional reaction to something, you are unlikely to get an honest answer because people think it is wrong to be emotional. But the term *red hat* is neutral. You can ask someone to 'take off the black hat for a moment' more easily than you can ask that person to stop being cautious. The neutrality of the colours allows the hats to be used without embarrassment. Thinking becomes a game with defined rules rather than a matter of exhortation and condemnation. The hats are referred to directly:

. . . I want you to take off your black hat.

. . . For a few minutes let us all put on our red thinking hats.

. . . That's fine for yellow hat thinking. Now let's have the white hat.

When you are dealing with people who have not read this book and who are unaware of the symbolism of the six thinking hats, the explanation attached to each colour can quickly give the flavour of each hat. You should then follow up by giving those people a copy of this book to read. The more widespread the idiom, the more efficient it will be in use. Eventually you should be able to sit down at any discussion table and switch in and out of 'hats' with ease.

Chapter 3
Using the Hats

There are two basic ways to use the hats. The hats can be used singly to request a type of thinking. Or, the hats can be used in a sequence to explore a subject or solve a problem.

Single Use

In single use, the hats are used as symbols to request a particular type of thinking. In the course of a conversation or discussion, you may come to a point where there is a need to generate some fresh options:

. . . I think we need some green hat thinking here.

Later in the same meeting, another course of action is suggested:

. . . Maybe we should have some black hat on this.

This artificiality of the hats is their great strength. Without the hats, our requests for thinking are both feeble and personal:

. . . We need some creativity here.

. . . Don't be so negative.

When Ron Barbaro was head of Prudential Insurance, I watched him interact with his executives. He would suggest an idea. Those around him would point out that the agents might not like it, that it might be risky, that it may not be legal, and so on. He would listen carefully and then say: 'Yes. That's fine black hat thinking. Now let's try the yellow hat.'

In Japan it is bad manners to criticize anything the boss might say. The hats provide a neutral signal that allows for cautious comments.

. . . Mr Shinto, I would like to do some black hat thinking here.

The red hat provides a unique opportunity to tap into the feelings, emotions and intuition of individuals. People usually do not put forward their feelings and as a manager, it is difficult to ask for feelings. But the formality and neutrality of the red hat make it possible to ask an individual for his or her feelings on a matter.

The yellow hat provides an opportunity to get people to look for values. An idea may be immediately dismissed because at first sight it has few virtues and many disadvantages. But after some directed yellow hat thinking, an idea may prove to have many benefits.

. . . This idea does not seem promising at all. But let's have some yellow hat on it.

It is usually harder to find benefits than dangers. Under the yellow hat there can be some powerful insights. Something that did not seem promising can in fact have a high value that had not been spotted before.

The white hat provides a means for getting people to separate pure information from judgement. The formality of the white hat asks someone to stick directly to the information.

It is not necessary to specify a hat every time you open your mouth. The hats are there for you to use at your discretion as a formal means to ask for a certain type of thinking. Once people have been trained in the use of the hats, they know exactly how to respond. Instead of the general and vague request to 'think about this', there is now a precise way to ask for a particular mode of thinking.

Sequence Use

The hats can also be used one after the other in a certain sequence.

Any hat can be used as often as you like.

There is no need to use every hat.

The sequence may be made up of two, three, four or more hats.

There are two broad types of sequence: evolving and preset.

With the evolving sequence, you choose the first hat (or the facilitator does). When that hat is completed, the next hat is chosen, and so on. For two reasons, I would not recommend this method unless you are experienced in using the Six Hats method. The first reason is that the members of the group may spend so much time arguing about which hat should be used next that there will be little time for thinking about the subject itself. The second reason is that whoever is choosing the sequence of the hats may be seen to be manipulating the meeting to get an outcome he or she desires. Before you are experienced in using the Six Hats method, it is better to stick to pre-set sequences.

A pre-set sequence is set up at the beginning of the meeting, under an initial blue hat. The sequence is laid out in advance and then followed. Minor variations are permitted, depending on output.

Discipline

Discipline is very important. Members of the group must stay with the hat that is indicated at that moment. A member of the group is not permitted to say: 'I want to put on my black hat here.' That would mean going back to the usual argument mode. Only the group leader, chairperson or facilitator can indicate a change of hat. The hats cannot be used to describe what you want to say. The hats indicate the direction in which to think. It is very important that this discipline be maintained. After using the method for a while, people find it much easier to stay with the specified hat.

Timing

How much time should be allowed under each hat? I prefer to set a short time. That forces people to concentrate on what they are trying to do and reduces aimless waffle. I would normally allow one minute per person present. So if there are four people in the meeting, then four minutes would be allowed under each hat. If genuine ideas are still being put forward after that time, I would extend the time. So if under the black hat 'concern' points were being raised, there is no need to say: 'Sorry, time's up.' You can extend the time as long as genuine points are being made.

It is much better to set a short time and to extend it rather than set a long time and have people sitting around wondering what to say.

The red hat is different from the other hats with regard to timing. Only a short time is needed to get the red hat feeling from each of those present since there should not be explanations or qualifications. The expression of feeling should be brisk and definite. Often as little as one minute is enough for everyone present to express his or her feelings.

Guidelines

There is no one right sequence to follow. Any sequence of hats that makes sense to you will work. Some sequences are appropriate for exploration, some for problem solving, for dispute settlement, for decision making, and so forth. Just as a carpenter has to get used to the feel and use of tools, so it is important to get used to setting up sequences and using them.

A blue hat should always be used both at the beginning and at the end of the session – like two bookends.

The first blue hat indicates

why we are here,
what we are thinking about,
the definition of the situation (or problem),
alternative definitions,
what we want to achieve,
where we want to end up,
the background to the thinking and
a plan for the sequence of hats to be used.

The final blue hat indicates

what we have achieved,
outcome,
conclusion,
design,
solution, and
next steps.

What follows the first blue hat depends on the nature of the thinking.

A red hat may be used immediately after the first blue hat. This is done in situations where it is believed that there are already strong feelings on the subject. The red hat is an opportunity to get those feelings out in the open right at the beginning.

Before the first elections in South Africa I was asked to teach the Six Hats method to the heads of the Peace Accord Committees who were responsible for solving local problems. They would often start their meetings with the red hat in order to give people a chance to express their feelings and emotions.

The initial red hat should not be used in certain situations. For instance, if the boss expresses his or her feelings, everyone may feel the need to agree with the boss. The initial red hat should also not be used if there are no pre-existing feelings. There is no point in asking people to adopt feelings so early.

In an assessment situation, it makes sense to put the yellow hat before the black hat. If, under the yellow hat, you cannot find much value to the idea, there is no point in proceeding further. On the other hand, if you find much value under the yellow hat and then proceed to the black hat and find many obstacles and difficulties, you will be motivated to overcome the difficulties because you have seen the benefits. But if you start off by seeing all the difficulties, then your motivation is totally different.

Sometimes you may want to put a red hat after the final blue hat. This final red hat reflects back on the 'thinking performance':

What do we feel about our thinking?
Are we happy with the outcome?
Did we do a good job?

These are only some of the guidelines. There is a fuller set of guidelines with specific sequences for different situations in the formal training sessions given by authorized trainers, where there is an opportunity to select and practise sequences.

In general, any sequence that makes sense as a 'thinking strategy' is valid and will work.

Group and Individual

The most striking benefits of the Six Hats method are seen in group discussions or conversations. In such situations the method provides a framework that is much more effective than argument or free discussion.

The hats may also be used by an individual thinking on his or her own. The sequenced framework reduces confusion and ensures that all aspects are fully covered.

The hats may also be used in reports or other communications. Again, this allows every aspect to be covered. In a report, the framework also allows all 'caution' aspects to be put forward without causing offence.

Individuals in Groups

Even when the Six Hats method is used for group meetings, the chairperson or facilitator still can ask individuals to do some individual thinking. That allows people to come up with more ideas. In a group discussion you are so busy listening to others that there may be little time to think.

. . . We are now switching to the yellow hat. I want you to spend two minutes thinking on your own before we open the discussion.

Such individual thinking is particularly useful with the green, yellow and black hats.

The chairperson may ask individuals to take some time for individual thinking even in the middle of a hat.

. . . Now I'd like you to do some green hat thinking on your own. I am not happy with the alternatives we have so far.

Although most groups sessions involve individuals freely expressing their ideas whenever they want (under the relevant hat), it is also possible to ask individuals specifically for their thinking.

. . . Mr Smith, we have not heard from you. What is your black hat thinking on this matter?

. . . I would like some yellow hat from you, Henrietta.

When a hat is introduced it is also possible to go around the group, individual by individual, to get each person's thinking under that hat. This is particularly useful when some individual thinking time has been allowed.

THE WHITE HAT

Think of paper. Think of a computer printout. The white hat is about information. When the white hat is in use, everyone focuses directly and exclusively on information.

What information do we have?
What information do we need?
What information is missing?
What questions do we need to ask?
How are we going to get the information we need?

The information can range from hard facts and figures that can be checked to soft information like opinions and feelings. If you express your own feeling, that is red hat, but if you report on someone else expressing a feeling, that is white hat.

When two offered pieces of information disagree, there is no argument on that point. Both pieces of information are put down in parallel. Only if it becomes essential to choose between them will the choice be made.

The white hat is usually used towards the beginning of a thinking session as a background for the thinking that is going to take place. The white hat also can be used towards the end of the session as a sort of assessment: Do our proposals fit in with the existing information?

The white hat is neutral. The white hat reports on the world. The white hat is not for generating ideas though it is permissible to report on ideas that are in use or have been suggested.

A very important part of the white hat is to define the information that is missing and needed. The white hat defines the questions that should be asked. The white hat lays out the means (such as surveys and questionnaires) for obtaining the needed information.

White hat energy is directed at seeking out and laying out information.

Chapter 4

The White Hat

Facts and Figures

> *Can you role-play being a computer?*
> *Just give the facts in a neutral and objective manner.*
> *Never mind the interpretation: just the facts, please.*
> *What are the facts in this matter?*

Computers are not yet emotional (though we shall probably have to make them emotional if they are to think intelligently). We expect a computer to show us the facts and figures on demand. We do not expect a computer to argue with us and to use its facts and figures only in support of its argument.

Too often the facts and figures are embedded in an argument. The facts are used for some purpose rather than presented as facts. Facts and figures can never be treated objectively when put forward as part of an argument.

So we badly need a switch that says: 'Just the facts please – without the argument.'

Unfortunately, Western thinking, with its argument habits, prefers to give a conclusion first and then to bring in the facts to support that conclusion. In contrast, in the map-making type of thinking that I am advocating, we have to make the map first and then choose the route. That means that we have to have the facts and figures first.

So white hat thinking is a convenient way of asking for the facts and figures to be put forward in a neutral and objective manner.

At one time a mammoth monopolies case was being pursued against International Business Machines in the United States. The case was eventually dropped – probably because it was realized that the US needed the strength of IBM in order to compete with the highly organized Japanese electronic competition. It has also been suggested that there was another reason for dropping the case. IBM provided so many documents (about seven million, I believe) that no court could cope with the volume. If the judge dies during the course of a case, the case has to start all over again. Since judges are not appointed until they are relatively old enough to be relatively wise, there was a very good chance of the judge dying in the course of the case. So the case was untriable unless a very young judge was appointed in order to make this case his or her whole career.

The point of this story is that it is possible to reply to a request for facts and figures with so much information that the asker is overwhelmed by the amount.

... If you want the facts and figures you can (expletive deleted) have them. All of them.

This sort of response is understandable because any attempt to simplify the facts could be seen as a selection of facts to make a particular case.

In order to avoid being drowned in information, the person requesting the white hat thinking can focus his or her request in order to draw forth the needed information.

... Give me your broad white hat thinking on unemployment.

. . . Now give me the figures for school-leavers six months after they have left school.

The framing of suitable focusing questions is part of the normal process of asking for information. Lawyers skilled in cross-examination do this all the time. Ideally, the witness should be wearing the white thinking hat and should answer the questions factually. Judges and courtroom lawyers might find the white hat idiom most convenient.

. . . As I said, he returned to his apartment at six-thirty in the morning because he had spent the whole night gambling.

. . . Mr Jones, did you actually see the defendant gambling on the night of 30 June, or did he tell you he had been gambling?

. . . No, Your Honour. But he goes gambling almost every night.

. . . Mr Jones, if you were wearing the white thinking hat, what might you have said?

. . . I observed the defendant returning to his apartment at six-thirty in the morning on 1 July.

. . . Thank you. You may stand down.

It has to be said that lawyers in a courtroom are *always* trying to make a case. Their questions are therefore framed to support their line of argument or to destroy the line of argument of the other side. This is, of course, exactly the opposite of white hat thinking. The role of the judge is a curious one.

In the Dutch legal system there is no jury. The three judges or assessors try to use pure white hat thinking in order to find out the facts of the case. Their task is to make the 'map' and then to pass judgement. This does not seem to be the case in England or the United States, where the judge is there to preserve the rules of evidence and then to respond to the evidence extracted by the lawyers either directly or by means of a jury.

So any person framing questions in order to extract information needs to be sure that he or she is using the white thinking hat *himself* or *herself*. Are you really trying to get the facts, or to build up a case for an idea forming in your head?

. . . Last year there was a twenty-five per cent increase in the sale of turkey meat in the US, due to the interest in dieting and the concern with health. Turkey meat is perceived as being 'lighter'.

. . . Mr Fitzler, I have asked you to put on your *white hat.* The fact is the twenty-five per cent increase. The rest is your interpretation.

. . . No, sir. Market research clearly shows that the reason people give for buying turkey meat is that they think it is lower in cholesterol.

. . . Well then you have two facts. Fact one: that turkey-meat sales have risen by twenty-five per cent in the last year. Fact two: some market research shows that people claim to buy turkey meat because of their concern with cholesterol.

The white hat gives a sort of direction to aim towards in dealing with information. We can aim to play the white hat role as well as possible. This means aiming to get the pure facts. It is obvious that the white hat role involves some skill – perhaps more than the other hats.

. . . There is a rising trend in the number of women smoking cigars.

. . . That is not a fact.

. . . It is. I have the figures here.

. . . What your figures show is that for each of the last three years the number of women smoking cigars has risen above the level for the previous year.

. . . Isn't that a trend?

. . . It could be. But that is an interpretation. To me a trend suggests something that is happening and will continue to happen. The figures are the fact. It may be that women are smoking more cigars because they are smoking more anyway – possibly due to increased anxiety. Or it may simply be that over the last three years cigarmakers have spent an unusual amount of money persuading women to smoke cigars. The first is a trend that could provide opportunities. The second is much less of an opportunity.

. . . I simply used the word *trend* to describe rising figures.

. . . That may be a fair use of the word *trend*, but there is the other use with the implication of an ongoing process. So it might be better to use pure white hat thinking and say: 'For the last three years the figures show an increase in the number of women smoking.' Then we can discuss what this means and what it may be due to.

In this sense white hat thinking becomes a discipline which encourages the thinker to separate quite clearly in his or her own mind what is fact and what is extrapolation or interpretation. It might be imagined that politicians would have considerable difficulty with white hat thinking.

Chapter 5

White Hat Thinking

Whose Fact Is It?

> *Is it a fact or a likelihood?*
> *Is it a fact or is it a belief?*
> *Are there any facts?*

Much of what passes for fact is simply a comment made in good faith or is a matter of personal belief at the moment. Life has to proceed. It is not possible to check out everything with the rigour demanded of a scientific experiment. So in practice we establish a sort of two-tier system: *believed facts* and *checked facts*.

We are certainly allowed to put forward believed facts under white hat thinking, but we must make it absolutely clear that these are second-class facts.

. . . I think I am right in saying that the Russian merchant fleet carries a significant part of world trade.

. . . I once read that the reason Japanese executives have such large expense accounts is that they give all their salary to their wives.

. . . I believe I am right in saying that the new Boeing 757 is much quieter than the previous generation of aircraft.

The irritated reader might point out that these 'weasel' phrases allow someone to say virtually anything and get away with it.

. . . Someone once told me that he had heard from a friend that Churchill secretly admired Hitler.

The way is open to allegation, gossip and hearsay. This is quite true. Nevertheless, we do have to have a way of putting forward believed facts.

The important point is the *use* to which the facts are to be put. Before we act upon a fact or make it the basis for a decision, we do need to check it. So we assess which of the believed facts could be useful and then proceed to try to verify it. For example, if the believed quietness of the Boeing 757 is vital to the siting of an airport, then we certainly need to take that from the 'believed' status to the 'checked' status.

The key rule for white hat thinking is that something should not be put forward at a higher level than is actually the case. When the statement is properly framed as a belief, then the input is permissible. Keep in mind the two-tier system.

Let me repeat that we do definitely need the belief tier because the tentative, the hypothetical and the provocative are essential for thinking. They provide the frameworks which move ahead of the facts.

We come now to a rather difficult point. When does 'belief' become 'opinion'? I can 'believe' that the Boeing 757 is quieter. I can also 'believe' (opinion) that women smoke more because they are now under more stress.

Let me say at once that *your own opinion* is never permissible under white hat thinking. That would destroy the whole purpose of the white hat. You can, of course, report the actual opinion of someone else.

. . . It is Professor Schmidt's opinion that man-powered flight will never be possible.

Note very carefully that the belief level of fact simply means something which *you believe to be a fact* but have not yet checked out thoroughly. You might prefer to have the two tiers as

1 checked fact, and
2 unchecked fact (belief).

In the end it is the attitude that matters. When wearing the white hat, the thinker puts forward neutral 'ingredient' statements. These are laid on the table. There can be no question of using them to push a particular point of view. As soon as a statement seems to be used to further a point of view, it is suspect: the white hat role is being abused.

In time the white hat rules becomes second nature. The thinker no longer tries to sneak in statements in order to win arguments. There develops the neutral objectivity of a scientific observer or an explorer who notes carefully the different fauna and flora without any notion of a further use for them. The mapmaker's task is to make a map.

The white hat thinker lays out the 'specimens' on the table – like a schoolboy emptying his pockets of some coins, some chewing gum and a frog.

Chapter 6

White Hat Thinking

Japanese-Style Input

Discussion, argument and consensus.
If no one puts forward an idea, where do ideas come from?
Make the map first.

The Japanese never acquired the Western habit of argument. It may be that disagreement was too impolite or too risky in a feudal society. It may be that mutual respect and saving face are too important to allow the attack of argument. It may be that Japanese culture is not ego-based like Western culture: argument often has a strong ego base. The most likely explanation is that Japanese culture was not influenced by those Greek thinking idioms which were refined and developed by medieval monks as a means of proving heretics to be wrong. It seems odd to us that they do not argue. It seems odd to them that we cherish argument.

At a Western-style meeting the participants sit there with their points of view and in many cases the conclusion they wish to see agreed upon. The meeting then consists of arguing through these different points of view to see which one survives the criticism and which one attracts the most adherents.

Modifications and improvements do take place in the initial ideas. But it tends to be a matter of 'marble sculpture', that is to say starting with a broad block and then carving it down to the end product.

A Western-style consensus meeting is less fiercely argumentative because there are no outright winners or losers. The output is one that is arrived at by everyone and agreeable to everyone. This is more like 'clay sculpture': there is a core around which pieces of clay are placed and moulded to give the final output.

Japanese meetings are not consensus meetings.

It is hard for Westerners to understand that Japanese participants sit down at a meeting without any preformed ideas in their heads. The purpose of the meeting is to *listen.* So why is there not a total and unproductive silence? Because each participant in turn puts on the white hat and then proceeds to give his piece of neutral information. Gradually the map gets more complete. The map gets richer and more detailed. When the map is finished the route becomes obvious to everyone. I am not suggesting that this process takes place at just one meeting. It may be stretched out over weeks and months with many meetings involved.

The point is that no one puts forward a ready-made idea. Information is offered in white hat fashion. This information slowly organizes itself into an idea. The participants watch this happen.

The Western notion is that ideas should be hammered into shape by argument.

The Japanese notion is that ideas emerge as seedlings and are then nurtured and allowed to grow into shape.

The above is a somewhat idealized version of the contrast between Western argument and Japanese information input. It is my intention here to make this contrast rather than to follow those who believe that everything Japanese is wonderful and should be emulated.

We cannot change cultures. So we need some *mechanism*

that will allow us to override our argument habits. The white hat role does precisely this. When used by everyone during a meeting, the white hat role can imply: 'Let's all pretend to be Japanese at a Japanese meeting.'

It is to make this sort of switch in a practical manner that we need artificial devices and idioms like the white thinking hat. Exhortation and explanation have little practical value.

(I do not want to get into an explanation of why the Japanese are not more inventive. Invention can require an ego-based culture with cantankerous individuals able to persist with an idea that seems mad to all around. We can do it in a more practical manner with the deliberate provocations of lateral thinking, which I discuss elsewhere and also in the section on green hat thinking.)

Chapter 7

White Hat Thinking

Facts, Truth and Philosophers

> *How true is a fact?*
> *Of what value are the language games of philosophy?*
> *Absolute truths and 'by and large'.*

Truth and facts are not as closely related as most people seem to imagine. Truth is related to a word-game system known as philosophy. Facts are related to checkable experience. The practical-minded who are not much concerned with such matters can skip to the next chapter.

If every swan we happen to see is white, can we make the bold statement that 'all swans are white'? We can and we do. For the moment that statement is a true summary of our experience. In this sense it is also a fact.

The first black swan that we see makes the statement untrue. So we have switched from true to untrue with remarkable abruptness. Yet if we are looking at facts, one hundred white swan experiences are still set against one black swan experience. So as a matter of experienced fact we can say: 'most swans are white'; 'by and large swans are white'; 'slightly more than ninety-nine per cent of swans are white'.

This 'by and large' stuff is immensely practical (by and large children like ice cream; by and large women use cosmetics) but of no use at all to logicians. The 'all' is essential in the statement '*all* swans are white'. This is because logic has to move from one absolute truth to another. 'If this is true . . . then this follows . . .'

When we come across the first black swan, the statement 'all swans are white' becomes untrue. Unless we choose to call the black swan something else. Now it becomes a matter of words and definitions. If we choose to keep whiteness as an essential part of the definition of a swan, then the black swan is something else. If we drop whiteness as an essential part of the definition, then we can include the black swan and we base the definition of a swan on other features. It is the design and manipulation of such definitions that is the essence of philosophy.

White hat thinking is concerned with usable information. So the 'by and large' and 'on the whole' idioms are perfectly acceptable. It is the purpose of statistics to give these rather vague idioms some specificity. It is not always possible to collect such statistics, so we often have to use the two-tier system (belief, checked fact).

. . . By and large corporations that base their spending on extrapolated future sales run into trouble. (It is possible to point to a few companies that have done this and been successful.)

. . . Sales will tend to rise if prices are lowered. (When house prices rise there may actually be increased sales for reasons of speculation, fear of inflation and fear of being left behind.)

. . . If you work hard, you will be successful in life. (A lot of hard-working people are not particularly successful.)

The spectrum of likelihood might be expressed as follows:

Always true
Usually true
Generally true
By and large
More often than not
About half the time
Often
Sometimes true
Occasionally true
Been known to happen
Never true
Cannot be true (contradictory)

How far along this spectrum is it permissible to go with the white hat role? As before, the answer to that question lies in the framing of the information. For example, it can be useful to know things that happen only very occasionally.

. . . Measles is usually harmless, but it can *sometimes* be followed by secondary infections, such as ear infections.

. . . In *very rare cases* inoculation can be followed by encephalitis.

. . . When irritated this breed of dog *has been known* to snap at children.

Obviously there is a value in being aware of this sort of information. There is also a dilemma. In the second example given, people's perception of the danger of encephalitis following inoculation may be thousands of times greater than the actual statistical danger. So it can be important to give actual figures in order to avoid inadvertent misinformation.

Are anecdotes acceptable under white hat thinking?

. . . There was a man who fell out of an aeroplane without a parachute and survived.

. . . Ford is said to have designed the Edsel on the basis of market research and it was a total disaster.

These may indeed be statements of fact and as such the white hat thinker has the right to put them forward. They must be framed as 'anecdotes' or 'instances'.

. . . Designs based on market research can often fail. Take, for instance, the Edsel car, the design of which is said to have been based on market research. It was a total failure.

The above statement is not legitimate white hat thinking – unless there is much more support for the claim that designs based on market research fail. Cats can fall off roofs but that is not normal behaviour.

Exceptions stand out simply because they are exceptions. We notice black swans because they are usually in a tiny minority. We notice the man who survives a fall from an aircraft without a parachute because it is somewhat unusual. The Edsel is always referred to for the same reason.

The purpose of white hat thinking is to be practical. So we must be able to put forward all sorts of information. The key point is to frame it properly.

. . . All the experts predict that the interest rate will fall by the end of the year.

. . . I talked to four experts and each of them predicted that the interest rate will fall by the end of the year.

. . . I talked to Mr Flint, Mr Ziegler, Ms Cagliatto and Mr Suarez and all of them predicted that the interest rate will fall by the end of the year.

Here we see three levels of precision. Even the third level may not be good enough. I may want to know *when* you talked to these experts.

There is nothing absolute about white hat thinking. It is a direction in which we strive to get better.

Chapter 8

White Hat Thinking

Who Puts on the Hat?

Put on your own hat.
Ask someone to put on the hat.
Ask everyone to put on the white hat.
Choose to answer with the hat on.

Most situations are covered with the above statements. What it amounts to is that you can ask, be asked or choose.

. . . What went wrong with our sales campaign?

. . . To answer that I am going to put on my white hat. We reached thirty-four per cent of retailers. Of these only sixty per cent took the product. Of those who took the product forty per cent took two items on a trial basis. Of the people we spoke to seventy per cent said the price was too high. There are two competitive products on the market with lower prices.

. . . Now give me your red hat thinking.

. . . We have a poor product which is overpriced. We have a bad image in the market. The competition's advertising is better and there is more of it. We do not attract the best salespeople.

The 'feel' aspects of the red hat thinking may be more important in this instance. But these 'feel' aspects could not be put forward under the white hat except in reporting what potential customers had said.

. . . Let's start off by all putting on our white thinking hats and telling what we know about juvenile crime. What are the figures? Where are the reports? Who can give evidence?

. . . You have told me that you are going to order Prime computers. Could you give me your white hat thinking on that?

. . . I don't want your guesses on what would happen if we lowered our transatlantic fare to two hundred and fifty dollars. I want your white hat thinking.

It is clear that white hat thinking excludes such valuable things as hunch, intuition, judgement based on experience, feeling, impression and opinion. That is, of course, the purpose of having the white hat: to have a way of asking only for information.

. . . You have asked for my white hat thinking on why I am changing jobs. The salary is no better. The perks are no better. The distance from home is no different. The career prospects are the same. The type of job is identical. That is all I can say under the white hat.

Chapter 9

Summary of White Hat Thinking

Imagine a computer that gives the facts and figures for which it is asked. The computer is neutral and objective. It does not offer interpretations or opinions. When wearing the white thinking hat, the thinker should imitate the computer.

The person requesting the information should use focusing questions in order to obtain information or to fill in information gaps.

In practice there is a two-tier system of information. The first tier contains checked and proven facts – first-class facts. The second tier contains facts that are believed to be true but have not yet been fully checked – second-class facts.

There is a spectrum of likelihood ranging from 'always true' to 'never true'. In between there are usable levels such as 'by and large', 'sometimes', and 'occasionally'. Information of this sort can be put out under the white hat, provided the appropriate 'frame' is used to indicate the likelihood.

White hat thinking is a discipline and a direction. The thinker strives to be more neutral and more objective in the presentation of information. You can be asked to put on the white thinking hat or you can ask someone to put it on. You can also choose to put it on or to take it off.

The white (absence of colour) indicates neutrality.

THE RED HAT

Think of fire. Think of warmth. Think of feelings. Using the red hat gives you an opportunity to express feelings, emotions and intuition without any need to explain or to justify them.

In a normal business discussion you are not supposed to allow your emotions to enter in. They enter in anyway – you merely disguise them as logic. The red hat provides a unique and special opportunity for feelings, emotions and intuition to be put forward as such.

Intuition may be based on a lot of experience.

. . . I feel this is the right person for the job.

. . . I feel this is a risky venture.

. . . My intuition tells me that this explanation is too complex.

Those feelings are useful. However, intuition is not necessarily always right. Even the great Einstein's intuition was wrong when he dismissed Heisenberg's uncertainty principle.

Under the red hat a range of feelings can be expressed: enthusiastic, 'love it', 'like it', neutral, uncertain, doubtful, mixed, unhappy, 'don't like it', and so on. The expression of feeling may vary from culture to culture. In Japan, feelings are expressed in a very low-key way: 'I must think about it.'

In the United States, more robust feelings are expressed: 'That is a lousy idea.'

There is no need to explain or justify the feelings. Indeed, that should never be permitted by the chairperson. If people think that they have to validate their feelings, they will put forward only feelings that can be validated. So no explanation should be allowed. In every case, just express the feelings as they exist – at that moment. It may be that in twenty minutes' time the feelings will have changed. Sometimes it is useful to have a red hat towards the beginning of the meeting to assess feelings, and then another red hat towards the end to see if the feelings have changed.

The red hat is always applied to a specific idea or situation. The thinker is not permitted to change the idea.

If the request is 'Give me your red hat on contributions that are compulsory', then the thinker would not be permitted to say: 'I would like the idea if the contributions were voluntary.'

It must be made very clear what the red hat is being applied to. Otherwise there is confusion. If necessary, the chairperson can put forward different versions (modifications) of an idea and get a red hat on each version.

The red hat can also cover 'intellectual feelings', which are perfectly valid:

. . . I feel that the idea has potential.

. . . That idea is very interesting.

. . . The idea is very unusual.

The red hat is always done on an individual basis. Every

individual present at the meeting is asked in turn for his or her red hat feeling on the issue under discussion.

Individuals should not be allowed to say 'pass' when they are asked for their red hat feelings. They can use terms like *neutral*, *undecided*, *confused*, *doubtful* or *mixed*.

If feelings are defined as *mixed*, then the facilitator may ask what goes into the mix.

The purpose of the red hat is to express feelings as they exist – not to force a judgement.

Chapter 10

The Red Hat

Emotions and Feelings

> *The opposite of neutral, objective information.*
> *Hunches, intuitions, impressions.*
> *No need to justify.*
> *No need to give reasons or the basis.*

Red hat thinking is all about emotions and feelings and the non-rational aspects of thinking. The red hat provides a formal and defined channel for bringing these things out into the open – as a legitimate part of the overall map.

If emotions and feelings are not permitted as inputs in the thinking process, they will lurk in the background and affect all the thinking in a hidden way. Emotions, feelings, hunches and intuitions are strong and real. The red hat acknowledges this.

Red hat thinking is almost the exact opposite of white hat thinking, which is neutral, objective and free of emotional flavour.

. . . Don't ask me why. I just don't like this deal. It's terrible.

. . . I do not like him and I don't want to do business with him. That is all there is to it.

. . . I have a hunch that this bit of land behind the church is going to be worth a great deal in a few years' time.

. . . That design is hideous. It will never catch on. It is a huge waste of money.

. . . I have a soft spot for Henry. I know he is a conman and he certainly conned us. But he did it with style. I like him.

. . . My gut feeling is that this deal is never going to succeed. It is bound to end in expensive litigation.

. . . I sense that this is a no-win situation. We are damned if we do and damned if we don't. Let's get out of it.

. . . I don't think it is fair to withhold this information until after the deal has been signed.

Any thinker who wants to express feelings of this sort should reach for the red hat. This hat gives official permission for the expression of feelings that range from pure emotion to hunch.

Chapter 11

Red Hat Thinking

The Place of Emotions in Thinking

Do emotions muck up thinking, or are they part of it?
At what point do emotions come in?
Can emotional people be good thinkers?

The traditional view is that emotions muck up thinking. The good thinker is supposed to be cool and detached and not influenced by emotion. The good thinker is supposed to be objective and to consider the facts in their own right and not for their relevance to his or her emotional needs. It is even claimed, from time to time, that women are much too emotional to make good thinkers. It is said that women lack the detachment that is needed for good decisions.

Yet any good decision must be emotional in the end. I place the emphasis on that phrase *in the end.* When we have used thinking to make the map, our choice of route is determined by values and emotions. I shall return to this point later.

Emotions give relevance to our thinking and fit that thinking to our needs and the context of the moment. They are a necessary part of the operation of the brain, not an intrusion or some relic of the age of animal survival.

There are three points at which emotion can affect thinking.

There may be a strong background emotion such as fear, anger, hatred, suspicion, jealousy or love. This background limits and colours all perception. The purpose of red hat thinking is to make visible this background so that its subsequent influence can be observed. The whole of thinking may be dominated by such a background emotion. The background emotion may be attached to a person or a situation or it may be in place for other reasons.

In the second instance the emotion is triggered by the initial perception. You perceive yourself to have been insulted by someone and thereafter your whole thinking about that person is coloured by this feeling. You perceive (perhaps falsely) that someone is saying something out of self-interest and thereafter you discount everything that person says. You perceive something to be an advertisement and thereafter withhold belief. We are very quick to make these snap judgements and to become locked in to the emotions they release. Red hat thinking gives us an opportunity to bring such feelings directly to the surface as soon as they arise.

. . . If I were to put on my red hat, I would say that your offer could be seen as furthering your own interests rather than that of the company.

. . . My red hat thinking tells me you want to oppose the merger in order to preserve your job rather than to benefit the shareholders.

The third point at which emotions can come in is after a map of the situation has been put together. Such a map should also include the emotions turned up by red hat thinking. Emotions – including a great deal of self-interest – are then brought in to choose the route on the map. Every decision has a value base. We react emotionally to values. Our reaction to the value of freedom is emotional (especially if we have been deprived of freedom).

... Now that we have as clear a picture of the situation as we are likely to get, let's all put on our red thinking hats and give our emotional choice of action.

... Of the two choices – continue with the strike or negotiation – I prefer the first. I do not feel the time is right for negotiation. Neither side has been hurt enough to want to give up anything.

For those who see the value of expressing the emotions involved in thinking about a certain matter, the red hat idiom provides a useful means of legitimizing those emotions so that they can take their place on the final map.

But could red hat thinking ever draw out those emotions which must be kept hidden?

... I am opposing her appointment because I am jealous of her and her quick rise to power.

Would anyone ever really reveal such jealousy? Probably not. But the red hat idiom allows a way around this.

... I am going to put on my red hat and I am then going to say that I feel that opposition to the promotion of Anne may be based, in part, on jealousy.

Alternatively:

. . . I am going to take cover under my red hat and I am going to say that I am opposed to the promotion of Anne. It is just a feeling I have.

It should also be remembered that a thinker in the privacy of his or her own mind can choose to put on the red thinking hat. This allows the thinker to bring his or her emotions to the surface in a legitimate way.

. . . There could be an element of fear here. Fear of the hassle involved in changing jobs.

. . . Yes, I am very angry. And at the moment I just want to get my own back. I don't like being cheated.

. . . I have to admit that I am just not happy in this job.

Red hat thinking encourages the search: 'Just what are the emotions involved here?'

Chapter 12

Red Hat Thinking

Intuition and Hunches

How valid are intuitions?
How valuable are intuitions?
How are intuitions to be used?

The word *intuition* is used in two ways. Both are correct. But in terms of brain function they are totally different. Intuition can be used in the sense of a sudden insight. This means that something which was perceived in one way is suddenly perceived in another. This may result in creativity, a scientific discovery or a mathematical leap forward.

. . . Shift attention from the winner to all the losers and you will quickly see that 131 singles entrants will require 130 matches to produce 130 losers.

The other use of the word *intuition* is the immediate apprehension or understanding of a situation. It is the result of a complex judgement based on experience – a judgement that probably cannot be itemized or even expressed in words. When you recognize a friend you do so immediately, as a complex judgement based on many factors.

. . . I have an intuition that this electric car is just not going to sell.

Such an intuition may be based on knowledge of the market, experience with similar products and an understanding of buying decisions at this price range.

It is this 'complex' judgement type of intuition that I want to deal with here.

Intuition, hunch and feeling are close. A hunch is a hypothesis based on intuition. Feeling can range from a sort of aesthetic feeling (almost a matter of taste) to a defined judgement.

. . . I have the feeling that he will back down when it comes to the crunch.

. . . I have the strong feeling that this bus ticket and that bike are the vital clues in this murder hunt.

. . . I have the feeling that this is not the right theory. It is too complex and messy.

Successful scientists, successful entrepreneurs and successful generals all seem to have this 'feel' for situations. With an entrepreneur we say that he or she 'smells money'. This suggests that the profits are not obvious enough to be seen by everyone but that the entrepreneur with a specially developed sense of smell for money can detect them.

There is nothing infallible about intuition. In gambling, intuition is notoriously misleading. If red has come up eight times in a row at roulette, intuition strongly suggests that black will come up next. Yet the odds remain exactly the same. The table has no memory.

So how do we treat intuition and feeling?

First of all, we give them legitimacy with red hat thinking.

The red hat permits us to ask for feelings and also to express them as a proper part of thinking. Perhaps emotions and intuition should have separate hats, but that would only complicate matters. I believe it is possible to treat them together under the heading of 'feelings' even though their natures are different.

We can try to analyse the reasons behind an intuitive judgement, but we are unlikely to be totally successful. If we cannot spell out the reasons, should we trust the judgement?

It would be difficult to make a major investment on the basis of a hunch. It is best to treat intuition as part of the map.

Intuition can be treated as one might treat an adviser. If the adviser has been reliable in the past, we are likely to pay more attention to the advice offered. If intuition has been right on many occasions, we may be more inclined to listen to it.

. . . All the reasons are against lowering the price, but my intuition tells me it is the only way to recover market share.

An experienced property man develops a sense of opportunity. His accumulated experience is expressed as an intuition which tells him which deals to make and which ones to leave alone. That intuition exercised in the property field may be very valuable because it is derived from experience. But that property man's intuition applied to the outcome of a presidential election may not be so valuable.

Intuition can also be handled on a 'win some, lose some' basis. Intuition may not always be right, but if it has been right more often than wrong, then the overall result will be positive.

It would be dangerous to ascribe to intuition the infallibility of a mystic oracle. Yet intuition is a part of thinking. It is there. It is real. And it can contribute.

. . . Can you please red hat your intuition on this merger?

. . . My red hat feeling is that property prices are going to soar again quite soon.

. . . Give me a red hat on this new advertising campaign, will you?

. . . My red hat tells me this offer is not going to be accepted.

Where do intuition and opinion meet? We have seen that the white thinking hat does not permit the expression of opinion (though it may permit the reporting of the expressed opinions of others). This is because opinion is based on judgement, interpretation and intuition. The balance may be on the side of the judgement of known facts or on the side of feeling based on unknown factors. Opinions may be expressed under red, black or yellow hats. When the red hat is used, it is best to express an opinion as a feeling.

. . . My feeling is that boredom is responsible for much juvenile crime.

. . . My feeling is that the cinema box office wants a few spectaculars that are heavily promoted.

Chapter 13
Red Hat Thinking

Moment to Moment

> *Reacting and getting upset.*
> *This is what I feel about this meeting.*
> *To show or to hide feelings.*

Red hat feelings can be shown at any time in the course of a meeting, a discussion or a conversation. The feelings can be directed at the conduct of the meeting itself, not just the subject matter that is being discussed.

. . . I am going to reach for my red thinking hat and I am going to tell you all that I do not like the way this meeting is being conducted.

. . . I want to make a red hat statement. I feel we are being bullied into an agreement we do not want.

. . . Mr Hooper, my red hat view is that you never listen to anyone else.

. . . I have said what I wanted to say and now I am going to take off the red hat.

Set against the natural flow of emotions that takes place during any meeting, the red hat convention might seem artificial and unnecessary. Do you really have to 'put on' the red hat in order to be angry? Is it not possible to express emotions by means of looks and tone of voice?

It is exactly this *artificiality* that is the real value of the red hat. Normally emotions take some time to well up and even longer to die down. There is resentment and there is sulking. Offence is taken and offence is given. In a sense the red hat allows someone to switch in and out of the emotion mode in a matter of moments. You put on the red hat and you take it off. Views expressed under the red hat are less personal than views expressed without it, because it is recognized as being a formal idiom.

The very need to 'put on' the red hat reduces the amount of bickering. No one can be bothered to put on the red hat every time he or she thinks there has been some slight. And once the red hat idiom is established, putting forward emotional views without its formality comes to seem crude.

Because the red hat provides a definite channel for feelings and emotion, there is no longer a need to intrude at every point. Anyone who feels the need to be emotional has a defined way of doing so.

It is no longer necessary to try to guess the feelings of others. There is a means for asking them directly.

. . . I want you to put on your red hat and tell me what you think of my proposal.

. . . I suspect you don't like me. I want a red hat answer.

People in love like to hear their partners spell out the word even when they do not doubt the substance.

. . . Switching to a red hat level, I want to say that I am very pleased with the way this conference is going. Is that the general view?

. . . My feeling is that we all want to get this agreement settled and signed. Mr Morrison, can you red hat it for me from your point of view?

The red hat idiom should not be exaggerated or overused to the point of absurdity. It is totally unnecessary to formally adopt the idiom each time a feeling is expressed. The idiom is used only when a feeling is expressed or asked for in a defined and formal manner.

. . . If you make any more red hat statements, I am going to put your red hat out of reach.

. . . Can we have just one overall red hat statement from you, and then we'll leave it. What do you feel about this matter?

. . . I want just one opportunity to make a red hat statement. Then I am going to put away that hat and not use it again.

Chapter 14

Red Hat Thinking

The Use of Emotions

Can thinking change emotions?
The emotional background.
Emotions as bargaining positions.
Emotions, values and choices.

Once emotions have been made visible by means of the red hat idiom, then an attempt may be made to explore and even change them. This itself is no longer part of the red hat idiom.

Thinking can change emotions. It is not the logical part of thinking that changes emotions but the perceptual part. If we see something differently, our emotions may alter with the altered perception.

. . . Don't look at it as a defeat. Look at it as a powerful way of finding out the weaknesses and strengths of his tennis game.

. . . Would this offer be acceptable if it were to come as an initiative from your side?

. . . Write it off as an essential learning experience rather than an error in judgement. Learning is always expensive. We won't have to go through it again.

It is not always possible to provide perceptions that can alter emotions or make them evaporate. But it is always worth a try.

Expressed emotions can provide the constant background to the thinking or discussing. There is a constant consciousness of this emotional background. Decisions and plans are seen to be made against this background. From time to time it is useful to imagine a different emotional background and to see how things would be different.

. . . We all know that these negotiations are taking place against a background of extreme suspicion. Let us try to imagine what our thinking would be if each side really trusted the other side.

. . . There is a feeling that what we decide here is not going to make much difference. Events have taken over. Let us imagine that this is not so and that we do have it in our power to control things.

. . . We do have to be conscious of the background of anger that is present. We cannot ignore it.

As I have indicated earlier, emotions and feelings are part of the colouring on the map. By means of the red hat convention we can get to know those 'regions' which are highly coloured from an emotional point of view. In designing solutions to disputes we can then keep clear of such areas.

. . . The proposed restriction on your work for competing companies is obviously a sensitive point. We'll keep clear of that for the moment.

. . . The union executive is never going to agree to anything that comes across as a wage cut. That has been expressed forcibly enough.

Emotions are often used to establish bargaining positions. I do not refer to sulks, threats, blackmail or appeals for pity. I refer to the emotional value that is ascribed to certain matters. The principle of variable value is at the base of negotiation. Something has one value for one party and a different value for the other party. These values can be expressed directly by means of red hat thinking.

. . . The ability to cross union demarcation lines is very important to our productivity.

. . . We must insist that the proper disciplinary procedures be followed. We are not saying that Jones is innocent but the procedures laid down must be followed.

It is generally agreed that the ultimate purpose of any thinking must be the satisfaction of the thinker. So in the end the purpose of thinking is to satisfy the expressed emotions.

Difficulty arises on three counts. Does the proposed course of action really work out to satisfy the expressed desires?

. . . I do not feel that lowering prices will actually increase sales.

The second source of difficulty is when the satisfaction of the desires of one party is at the expense of the other party.

. . . We can increase the overtime or take on more workers. The first would benefit those already working. The second would benefit some of those now out of work.

The third source of difficulty is the conflict between short-term satisfaction and long-term satisfaction. A basic tenet of Christianity puts this very clearly: What does it profit a man if he gains the whole world but loses his soul?

. . . We can raise the advertising rates and get more revenue immediately. But long term we shall be driving advertisers to use other media.

. . . If we lower the price to attract customers from other airlines, we may get a temporary advantage. Then they will match our price and we may lose those customers again. But the lowered profitability will remain.

. . . I would really enjoy eating this plateful of French fries, but it is not going to help my weight problem.

. . . I am going to put money into this play because I like Nerida, who is playing the leading part, and I want to see a lot more of her.

. . . I want to be seen as willing to back exciting new technology ventures, but long term I know that steady growth is what my investors want.

Emotions are part of both the method of thinking and the matter to be thought about. It is no use hoping they will go away and leave the field to pure thinking.

Chapter 15

Red Hat Thinking

The Language of Emotions

Emotions do not have to be logical or consistent.
Emotions can be fine-tuned with language to match.
Resist the temptation to justify emotions.

The most difficult thing about wearing the red thinking hat is resisting the temptation to justify an expressed emotion. Such justification may be true or it may be false. In both cases red hat thinking makes it unnecessary.

. . . Never mind why you mistrust him. You mistrust him.

. . . You like the idea of an office in New York. There is no need to go into the details of why you like the idea. That could come later when we are nearer to a decision on the matter.

We are brought up to apologize for emotions and feelings because they are not the stuff of logical thinking. That is why we tend to treat them as an extension of logic. If we dislike someone, there must be a good reason for this. If we like a project, this must be based on logic. Red hat thinking frees us from such obligations.

Does this mean that we are free to have and to hold any prejudices we like? Is there not immense danger in this? On the contrary. There may be more danger in prejudices which are apparently founded in logic than in those which are acknowledged as emotions.

I am not opposed to the exploration of emotions and a probing for their foundation. But that is not part of the red hat idiom.

Emotions are fickle and often inconsistent. A questionnaire asked Americans whether they were in favour of involvement in Central America. The majority favoured involvement. Yet there was a majority against every single suggested method of involvement. It is possible to be in favour of involvement in the abstract but against it when the abstract is translated into concrete terms. Logically this may not make sense, but in the world of the emotions it does make sense.

The red hat convention is not a trumpet for the emotions, although some people may be tempted to use it in that way. It more closely resembles a mirror which reflects the emotions in all their complexity.

It is said that the Inuit (Eskimo) people have twenty words for snow. There are cultures that have as many words for the various nuances of love. English and many European languages do not have a wide range of emotion-indicating words in common usage. There are like/dislike, hate/love, pleased/not pleased, happy/unhappy. For example, we could use a word to indicate undecided-positive and another for undecided-negative. The word *suspicious* is rather too heavily negative.

Because red hat thinking allows us to be bold and open about our feelings, we can seek to fine-tune them to match the situation. Without the red hat we tend to be limited to the stronger words supplemented with tone and facial expression.

. . . I have a sense of your hesitancy on this deal. You do not want in, but you do not want to be left out either. You want to be on call in an antechamber. Ready to come in when it suits you.

. . . You don't dislike Morgan, but you feel uneasy about him. You would dearly like to have a good excuse to dislike him.

. . . We are simply out of tune on this matter.

. . . There is a sense of quiet deflation about this venture. Not a loss of enthusiasm but rather something resembling a very slow leak in an inflated rubber dinghy. You cannot see anything happening, but when you look again after a passage of time, it is clearly more flabby than before.

The red hat gives a thinker the liberty to be more of a poet with his or her feelings. The red hat offers feelings the right to be made visible.

Chapter 16

Summary of Red Hat Thinking

Wearing the red hat allows the thinker to say: 'This is how I feel about the matter.'

The red hat legitimizes emotions and feelings as an important part of thinking.

The red hat makes feelings visible so that they can become part of the thinking map and also part of the value system that chooses the route on the map.

The red hat provides a convenient method for a thinker to switch in and out of the feeling mode in a way that is not possible without such a device.

The red hat allows a thinker to explore the feelings of others by asking for a red hat view.

When a thinker is using the red hat, there should *never* be any attempt to justify the feelings or to provide a logical basis for them.

The red hat covers two broad types of feeling. First, there are the ordinary emotions such as fear and dislike to the more subtle ones such as suspicion. Second, there are the complex judgements that go into such types of feeling as hunch, intuition, sense, taste, aesthetic feeling and other not visibly justified types of feeling. Where an opinion has a large measure of this type of feeling, it can also fit under the red hat.

THE BLACK HAT

The black hat is the most used of all the hats. The black hat is perhaps the most important hat. The black hat is the hat of caution. The black hat is for being careful. The black hat stops us doing things that are illegal, dangerous, unprofitable, polluting, and so on.

The black hat is the hat of survival. An animal has to learn which berries are poisonous and to read the danger signs of a predator. In order to survive we need to be cautious. We need to know what to avoid. We need to identify what is not going to work. That is how we survive. One silly mistake and we could be wiped out no matter how creative we might be.

The black hat is the basis of Western civilization because the black hat is the basis of critical thinking. The basis of traditional argument has been to point out how something is contradictory or inconsistent. The black hat points out how something does not fit our resources, our policy, our strategy, our ethics, our values, and so forth.

The black hat is based on a natural mechanism in the mind. That is the 'mismatch' mechanism. The brain forms patterns of expectation: this is what the world is like. If we come across something that does not match these existing patterns, then we feel very uncomfortable. This natural mechanism ensures that we do not make mistakes.

Food is excellent. Food is essential for life. But too much food might make you overweight and might cause health problems. That is not the fault of the food but the fault of overeating.

In the same way, there are people who overuse the black hat and who spend all their time trying to find fault. The fault is not in the black hat but in the abuse, overuse or misuse of the black hat.

One of the great values of the Six Hats method is that there is an allotted time in which everyone is invited to be as cautious, as careful and as critical as possible. But outside this allotted time it is not permitted to be critical at every possible point.

Experience has shown that people who are habitually cautious and have built their reputations on being critical actually welcome the Six Hats method. The black hat allows them to use their critical abilities to the fullest. When there is a switch to another hat, then that thinker is given permission to move away from being cautious. In many cases cautious thinkers have surprised themselves by being very creative under the green hat.

Chapter 17

The Black Hat

Cautious and Careful

How something does not fit our experience.
Why something may not work.
Pointing out difficulties and problems.
Staying within the law.
Keeping to values and ethics.

The black hat is the 'natural' hat of the Western thinking tradition. With the black hat we point out what is wrong, what does not fit, and what will not work. It protects us from wasting money and energy. It protects us from doing silly things and from breaking the law.

Black hat thinking is always logical. There must always be a logical basis for the criticism. If the comment is purely emotional, then it comes under the red hat, not the black hat.

. . . I don't like the idea of lowering prices.

. . . That is red hat thinking. I want you to give me your black hat thinking. I want your logical reasons.

. . . Very well. In our past experience – which I can put in front of you as sales figures – lowering prices has not resulted in sufficient sales to offset the reduction in profit margin. Also, our competitors have a history of reducing prices to match the competition.

Black hat reasons must be capable of standing on their own. They must make sense. They must be reasonable in cold print and not only when presented by a persuasive person.

Black hat thinking is not balanced. Under the black hat the brain is sensitized to seek out possible danger, problems and obstacles. The focus is on why something may not work or may not be the right thing to do. The other side is presented under the yellow hat.

It has been suggested that there should be just one hat called *judgement.* Under this hat the thinker would look for the pros and cons of a situation or solution. Although this may work in philosophy, it does not work in practice. The brain can be sensitized in only one direction at a time.

The specificity of the black hat relieves the thinker of the need to be fair and to see both sides of the matter at the same time. Under the black hat the thinker is encouraged to be as cautious as possible. Under the yellow hat the thinker sets out to look for benefits. You cannot do both effectively at the same time.

As with the other hats, the black hat comments always depend on a particular context: 'This car is capable of doing only fifty miles per hour.'

What sort of comment is that?

It could be a comment under the white hat because it is a simple statement of fact.

It could also be a comment under the black hat. In a general sense, we do expect cars to go faster than that. In a specific sense, if we are in a hurry to get somewhere, then this is very much a black hat observation.

There may be circumstances, however, where it actually could be a yellow hat comment. This might be a first car for a youngster who is just learning to drive. The fact that it can do only fifty miles per hour may be an advantage since the risk of a serious accident is thereby reduced.

The black hat legitimizes the value and importance of caution.

. . . I can see that this idea is very attractive. We have considered all the benefits. I do think we need some black hat thinking here. We need to know the potential dangers and difficulties. What is the downside?

. . . We need to be aware of the possible dangers in order to be on the lookout for them. We need some black hat thinking here.

. . . I am all in favour of appointing Peter to this post. But it would be sensible to have some black hat thinking first.

. . . Sales have risen dramatically after that advertising campaign. Is there anything we need to be cautious about? Let's have some black hat thinking.

. . . We both like this house very much. That is strong red hat thinking. Let's try the black hat for a moment or two.

The black hat gives a proper place to cautious thinking. By endorsing and legitimizing caution, the black hat also indicates that it is just one mode of thinking. It should be used properly and effectively.

In order to get the full value from any suggestion or idea, it is important that the black hat be done thoroughly. This helps both in the assessment of the idea and in the design of the idea.

In its assessment role the black hat helps someone decide whether to go ahead with the idea or to abandon it. The final decision is based on a combination of white hat (facts), yellow hat (benefits), black hat (caution) and red hat (intuition and feeling).

In its 'design' role, the black hat points out the weaknesses in an idea so that those weaknesses can be put right.

. . . This seems an excellent idea. Let's have a strong black hat effort to find out the weaknesses so that we can do something about those weaknesses right now, at the design stage, rather than find out about them too late.

. . . We have decided on this course of action. We need to lay out all the potential problems, obstacles and difficulties so that we can plan how to overcome them. So we need the black hat.

Chapter 18

Black Hat Thinking

Content and Process

> *Point out errors in thinking.*
> *Question the strength of the evidence.*
> *Does the conclusion follow?*
> *Is it the only possible conclusion?*

A great deal of traditional Western argument attacks the process of the argument: if the process is incorrect, then the conclusion cannot be correct. In fact, the conclusion can indeed be correct, but has not been proved to be correct.

Because the Six Hats method is so different from argument there is no need for detailed discussion of process. Nevertheless, under the black hat it is possible to point out deficiencies in the thinking process itself.

. . . That remark you made is an assumption, not a fact.

. . . Your conclusion does not follow from what you have been telling us.

. . . Those figures are not the ones you showed last time.

. . . That is only one possible explanation. But it is by no means the only one.

It would destroy the value of the whole method if a person were allowed to interrupt at any point with those sorts of comments. We would be back to the limitations of the argument mode. So the thinker should note and accumulate the main points of criticism and put them forward only when the black hat is in use.

Under the white hat someone puts forward a set of sales figures. One person present knows that the figures are actually five years old. Should that person interrupt and point out the error? It would be better to lay out another white hat point.

. . . The figures you have been given are five years old. We do not have more up-to-date figures.

Because the Six Hats method is very different from argument, the rules of argument do not apply. It is no longer a matter of arguing from one point to another but of filling the field with possibilities.

. . . If we increase prison sentences and penalties, we will reduce crime.

That seems a logical enough deduction, but it may not be valid in practice. If the risk of getting caught is actually very low, or is perceived to be very low, then the increase in punishment may have little effect. It is also possible that crime could get more violent: a criminal may now be inclined to kill a victim to remove the witness. Also, longer stays in prison might turn casual criminals into hardened criminals through the influence of the inmates.

These are all possibilities. Far too often proof is no more than lack of imagination.

If there were actual white hat figures to show that increased penalties reduced crime in the long-term as well as in the short-term, then those figures would be more valuable than apparently logical deduction.

. . . Holiday travel is likely to increase because family incomes are increasing, airfares are going down, travel is better organized and there may be fewer children.

. . . It is possible that people will get bored with travel. Technology might provide new ways of being entertained at home. Diseases in far-off places might discourage travel.

Those possibilities are laid down alongside each other, as in parallel thinking. Parallel thinking lays out different viewpoints and disagreements.

Logical deduction insists on certainty. The Six Hats method deals with possibilities and likelihood. In the real world it is very difficult to be certain. Action has to be taken on 'likelihood'.

. . . That is indeed a possibility. But you have not proved it as a certainty.

There are indeed times when matters can be dealt with in a cut-and-dried, logical fashion. The bulk of practical thinking, however, is on the basis of likelihood.

Although it is very tempting, the black hat is not permission to go back to 'argument'. Procedural errors can be pointed out. Parallel statements that express a differing point of view can be laid down. In the end there should be a clear map of possible problems, obstacles, difficulties and dangers. These can be clarified and elaborated.

Under the green hat an attempt is made to overcome or cope with the difficulties suggested under the black hat.

To begin with, people do find it hard not to jump in to disagree with a point that has just been made. It is up to the chairperson or facilitator to maintain the hat discipline.

Chapter 19

Black Hat Thinking

The Past and the Future

> *What is likely to happen in the future?*
> *Does this fit past experience?*
> *What are the risks?*

A very important function of the black hat is risk assessment. All proposed actions are going to be carried out in the future. This is an extremely important difference between 'academic' thinking and 'real world' thinking. In academic thinking it is enough to describe, to analyse and to offer explanations. In the real world there is the action element – which I sometimes call *operacy*.

What will happen if we take this action?
Will it be acceptable?
Do we have the resources to do it?
How will people react?
How will competitors react?
What can go wrong?
What are the potential problems?
Will it continue to be profitable?

We have to base speculations about the future on our own experience and on the experience of others.

. . . In times of inflation people save more.

. . . In times of inflation people save less.

Both statements are correct. Where there is a past history of inflation people save less because they know that money becomes worthless. Where there is no such history they may start by saving more because they feel they need more money. Where there is a high level of financial sophistication people may choose to borrow rather than save because the ultimate interest rate may be negative.

. . . After twenty years in the cosmetics business, I want to say that in my experience you cannot have the same brand both as a premium product and also a commodity product. It will not work.

. . . In the hotel business the same basic product can be branded differently and put in a very different price bracket. This has proved successful.

Both points of view are valid based on experience. One would be put forward under the black hat and the other under the yellow hat. In practice, the yellow hat comment could also be put forward under the black hat as a challenge to the cosmetics statement: 'That is not necessarily true because in the hotel business . . .'

In looking into the future and using lessons from the past, the question is always whether that particular lesson is relevant. Are the circumstances the same?

. . . That branding policy may hold true for hotels where you do not directly experience two products at the same time. But it might not hold true for a breakfast cereal.

One way of putting forward comments under the black hat is to say: 'I see a danger . . .'

. . . I see a danger that the competition will match our lower prices.

. . . I see a danger of overproduction of milk.

. . . I see a danger that a new company will offer no-frills insurance.

. . . I see a danger in overpricing our wines because many countries around the world are now producing excellent wines.

Chapter 20

Black Hat Thinking

The Problem of Overuse

It is easy to be critical.
Some people enjoy being only critical.
The need to contribute.

As I indicated earlier, the black hat is an excellent hat. But like many excellent things, it can be overused and abused. Pasta is an excellent food but if you had pasta every day for every meal, you would not be so enthusiastic about pasta.

It is much easier to be critical than to be constructive. It is hard to design a chair. Criticizing a chair is much easier. If the chair is simple, then you criticize it as being old-fashioned or boring. If the chair is elaborate, then you criticize it as being vulgar or pretentious. By deliberately choosing a concept that is different from the one presented it is always possible to criticize – if you are so inclined.

There are people whose self-importance and self-image are based on their willingness to criticize. In a meeting, people want to be involved, to be noticed, to contribute, and the easiest sort of contribution is the 'Yes . . . but' type of contribution. If 95 per cent of the idea is excellent, the tendency is to focus on the less excellent 5 per cent. That is useful at the design stage because the faulty 5 per cent can be put right. It is less useful at the assessment stage when the excellent 95 per cent should be acknowledged.

Overuse of the black hat is not helpful. Sometimes it is

simply ego-driven. Someone who is incapable of making any other sort of comment is limited to critical comments. Most often it is just habit. In the argument habit it is permissible to make negative comments at any point.

Once people get used to the Six Hats framework they often change out of the 'permanent caution' mode. They perform well under the black hat – but now they also perform well under the yellow hat and the green hat. They come to welcome this opportunity to show their ability in more modes than just one.

It is important to recognize the excellence and importance of the black hat and to refrain from overuse of the black hat.

Chapter 21

Summary of Black Hat Thinking

Black hat thinking is concerned with caution. At some stage we need to consider risks, dangers, obstacles, potential problems and the downside of a suggestion. It would be extremely foolish to proceed with any suggestion unless full consideration has been given to the caution aspect. The black hat is about being careful. The black hat seeks to avoid dangers and difficulties. The black hat points out matters that need attention because they may be weak or harmful. The black hat draws us to matters that need our attention.

The black hat can be used as part of assessment: should we proceed with this suggestion?

The black hat is used in the design process: what are the weaknesses that we need to overcome?

The black hat seeks to lay out the risks and potential problems in the future: what may go wrong if we implement this suggestion?

The black hat is very much about 'fit'. Does this suggestion fit our past experiences? Does this suggestion fit our policy and strategy? Does this suggestion fit our ethics and values? Does this suggestion fit our resources? Does this suggestion fit the known facts and the experience of others?

Under the black hat we focus directly on the 'caution' aspects. This is the basis of survival, of success and of civilization.

Black hat thinking may point out procedural errors in the thinking itself. But black hat thinking is not argument and must not be allowed to degenerate into argument. The purpose of black hat thinking is to put the caution points on the map.

Black hat thinking can be abused and overused if it is the only mode of thinking. This abuse in no way diminishes the value of the black hat, just as the dangerous and reckless driving of a car does not mean that cars are dangerous.

THE YELLOW HAT

Think of sunshine. Think of optimism. Under the yellow hat a thinker deliberately sets out to find whatever benefit there may be in a suggestion. Under the yellow hat the thinker tries to see how it may be possible to put the idea into practice.

The yellow hat is a harder hat to wear than the black hat. There is a natural mechanism in the brain that helps us to avoid dangers. There is no such natural mechanism for the yellow hat. For this reason most people are much better at using the black hat than the yellow hat.

We need to develop 'value sensitivity'. That means being as sensitive to value as we already are sensitive to danger. That is a habit that has to be developed. I have sat in on many creative meetings where excellent ideas have been generated. Unfortunately, the people present do not see the value in their own ideas. It is a waste of time setting out to be creative if you are not going to recognize a good idea. That is why the development of value sensitivity is so very important.

The yellow hat has a high value because it forces people to spend time seeking out value. Sometimes there are big surprises under the yellow hat. Something that did not seem very interesting suddenly has a high value. Even the most unattractive ideas can be found to have some value, if we look hard enough.

The yellow hat should be logically based. There should be some reason given for the value put forward. The yellow hat is a judgement hat and is not based on fantasy. What are the values? For whom? Under what circumstance? How are the values delivered? What other values are there?

Chapter 22

The Yellow Hat

Speculative-Positive

> *Positive thinking.*
> *Yellow is for sunshine and brightness.*
> *Optimism.*
> *Focus on benefit.*
> *Constructive thinking and making things happen.*

Being positive is a choice. We can choose to look at things in a positive way. We can choose to focus on those aspects of a situation that are positive. We can search for benefits.

Negative thinking may protect us from mistakes, risk taking and danger. Positive thinking has to be a mixture of curiosity, pleasure, greed and the desire to 'make things happen'. It could be argued that man's progress depends on this desire to make things happen. In my book about success, *Tactics: The Art and Science of Success*, the one thing that characterized successful people was this overwhelming desire to make things happen.

I have termed the yellow hat 'speculative-positive' because with any plan or action we are looking forward into the future. That is where the action or plan is going to be worked out. We can never be as certain about the future as we are about the past, so we have to speculate as to what might happen. We set out to do something because it is worth doing. It is our assessment of this 'worth' or value that provides the 'positive' aspect of speculative-positive.

Even when we look at something that has happened, we can choose to look at the positive aspects or extract a positive interpretation.

. . . The positive thing is that now we know how he is going to act. The uncertainty is over.

. . . Let's put on our yellow hats and look at the positive aspects. Kodak has decided to go into the instant-camera market. So they will have to advertise their products. That will increase the public's awareness of the merits of instant photography. That should help our sales – especially if the public perceives that our product is better.

. . . Failing that examination was the best thing that could have happened to her. She would not have been happy as a teacher.

For a few people, being positive is a natural habit of mind. Most people will be positive when they are putting forward an idea of their own. Most people will be positive about an idea if they immediately see something in it for themselves. Self-interest is a strong basis for positive thinking. The yellow thinking hat does not have to await such motivations. The yellow thinking hat is a deliberate device which the thinker chooses to adopt. The positive aspect is not the result of seeing merit in the idea but precedes this. The yellow hat comes first. The thinker puts on the yellow hat and then follows its *requirements* to be positive and optimistic.

In the printing analogy that I used earlier, the yellow hat puts on the yellow colour just as the red hat puts on the red colour.

. . . Before you do anything else I want you to put on your yellow hat and tell me what you think about this new approach.

. . . You have told me all the reasons why you do not like the idea and why it will probably fail. Now I want you to put your yellow thinking hat firmly in place. What do you see now?

. . . From a yellow hat point of view, can you see any merit in making this fitting out of plastic instead of metal? The cost would be about the same.

. . . I have this idea of selling potato chips in a twin pack. No one seems to like it. Will you yellow hat it for me?

. . . I do not want a balanced view or an objective view. I want a definite yellow hat view.

. . . My black hat tells me that this new cheap lighter could hurt our sales. But my yellow hat tells me that the cheap lighter could kill the middle market and force some buyers up to the expensive market and so benefit us.

. . . It is hard to wear a yellow hat at the moment. But the newspaper strike could make people realize how much they missed their papers and how newspapers are much better than television for some things.

Although yellow hat thinking is positive, it requires just as much discipline as the white hat or the black hat. It is not just a matter of making a positive assessment of something that turns up. It is a deliberate search for the positive. Sometimes this search is futile.

. . . I am wearing my yellow thinking hat but I cannot find anything positive to say.

. . . I will put on my yellow hat but I do not expect to find anything positive.

It may be claimed that unless a positive aspect is obvious, it cannot really be worth much. It may be claimed that there is no point in cudgelling one's brain to find remote positive points that will have little practical value. This is to misunderstand perception. There may be very powerful positive points that are not at all obvious at first sight. That is how entrepreneurs work. They see the value that those around them have not yet spotted. Value and benefit are by no means always obvious.

Chapter 23

Yellow Hat Thinking

The Positive Spectrum

When is optimism foolishness?
From the hopeful to the logical.
What is realism?

There are people who will think well of a conman even after he has deceived them. They feel that he was sincere at the time and that he was let down by events or colleagues. They remember his persuasiveness and how they enjoyed being persuaded.

There are Pollyanna-type people who are optimistic to the point of foolishness. There are people who seriously *expect* to win major prizes in a lottery and seem to base their lives on this hope. There are industrialists who look at the huge aspirin market and feel that if they could only get a tiny part of it, it would be well worthwhile.

At what point does optimism become foolishness and foolish hope? Should yellow hat thinking have no restraints? Should yellow hat thinking take no account of likelihood? Should that sort of thing be left to black hat thinking?

The positive spectrum ranges from the over-optimistic at one extreme to the logical-practical at the other. We have to be careful how we handle this spectrum. History is full of impractical visions and dreams which inspired the effort that eventually made those dreams a reality. If we restrict our yellow hat thinking to what is sound and well known, there is going to be little progress.

The key point is to look at the action that follows the optimism. If that action is to be no more than hope (like the hope of winning a lottery prize or the hope that some miracle will rescue the business), then such optimism may be misplaced. If the optimism is going to lead to some action in the chosen direction, it becomes more difficult. Over-optimism usually leads to failure, but not always. It is those who expect to succeed who do succeed.

. . . There is a remote chance that someone survived the crash-landing on the glacier. We must go and look.

. . . It is possible that this new party will split the opposition vote.

. . . If we invest heavily in promoting this film, we should have a success on our hands.

. . . There is a chance it will be chosen car of the year. We should be prepared to follow that up in our publicity. It may not happen but we have to be ready.

As with the other thinking hats, the purpose of the yellow hat is to colour the notional thinking map. For this reason optimistic suggestions should be noted and put on the map. There is no need to assess them in detail before putting them on the map. Nevertheless, it is worth labelling such suggestions with a rough estimate of likelihood.

A simple likelihood classification can be drawn up:

Proven
Very likely, based on experience and what we know
Good chance – through a combination of different things
Even chance
No better than possible
Remote or long shot

This is somewhat similar to the one used for white hat thinking.

We may choose never to back a long shot, but that long shot needs to be on the map. If it is on the map, we have the choice of rejecting it or trying to improve the odds. If it is not put on the map, we have no choice at all.

. . . I know he is very busy and very expensive but get in touch with him and invite him to open the conference. He may just accept. At worst he can only say no.

. . . Every girl wants to be an actress and only a very few succeed, so the chances of success are not great. However, some people do make it, so try if you want to.

. . . You are not likely to find any hidden art treasure in a village antique shop. But then most hidden art treasures were in places no one expected to find them.

Chapter 24
Yellow Hat Thinking

Reasons and Logical Support

What is the positive view based upon?
Why do you think it will happen this way?
Background reasons for the optimism.

A positive assessment may be based on experience, available information, logical deduction, hints, trends, guesses and hopes. Does the yellow hat thinker have to spell out the reasons for his or her optimism?

If no reasons are given, the 'good feeling' may just as well be placed under the red hat as a feeling, hunch or intuition. Yellow hat thinking should go much further.

Yellow hat thinking covers positive judgement. The yellow hat thinker should do his or her best to find as much support as possible for the proffered optimism. This effort should be conscientious and thorough. *But yellow hat thinking need not be restricted to those points that can be fully justified.* In other words, there should be a full effort to justify the optimism, but if that effort is not successful, the point can still be put forward as a speculation.

The emphasis of yellow hat thinking is on exploration and positive speculation. We set out to find the possible benefits. Then we seek to justify them. This justification is an attempt to strengthen the suggestion. If this logical support is not provided under the yellow hat, it is not going to be provided anywhere else.

. . . My yellow hat thinking suggests that omelettes would make good fast-food items. If I look around for reasons to support that view, I might pick on diet consciousness and the preference for light foods. I might also say that as people tend not to have eggs for breakfast any longer, there is room to have eggs at other times.

. . . What about a range of action gloves? Not just gloves to keep you warm but gloves for working on the car, gloves for eating with, gloves for housework. People must do more for themselves today. They are also becoming more conscious of appearance and skin care.

Chapter 25
Yellow Hat Thinking
Constructive Thinking

Making things happen.
Proposals and suggestions.

Imagine eight brilliant critical thinkers sitting around a table to consider means to improve the town's water supply. None of those brilliant minds can get started until someone puts forward a proposal. Now the full brilliance of that critical training can be unleashed. But where does the proposal come from? Who has been trained to put forward the proposal?

Critical thinking is a very important part of thinking, but it is by no means sufficient. What I so strongly object to is the notion that it is enough to train critical minds. This has been the tradition of Western thinking and it is inadequate.

Black hat thinking covers the aspect of critical thinking. When dealing with the black thinking hat, I made it quite clear that a thinker wearing the black hat should play this role to the full: he or she should be as fiercely critical as possible. This is an important part of thinking and it should be done well.

It is to yellow hat thinking that the constructive and generative aspect is left. It is from yellow hat thinking that ideas, suggestions and proposals are to come. We shall see later that the green hat (creativity) also plays an important role in designing new ideas.

Constructive thinking fits under the yellow hat because all

constructive thinking is positive in attitude. Proposals are made in order to make something *better*. It may be a matter of solving a problem. It may be a matter of making an improvement. It may be a matter of using an opportunity. In each case the proposal is designed to bring about some positive change.

One aspect of yellow hat thinking is concerned with reactive thinking. This is the positive assessment aspect, which is the counterpart of the black hat negative assessment. The yellow hat thinker picks out the positive aspects of an idea put before him or her just as the black hat thinker picks out the negative aspects. In this section I am dealing with a different aspect of yellow hat thinking – the constructive aspect.

. . . To improve the water supply we could build a dam on the Elkin River, thereby creating a reservoir.

. . . There is abundant water in the mountains fifty miles away. Would it be feasible to put in a pipeline?

. . . Normal flushing toilets use about eight gallons every time they are flushed. There are new designs that use only one gallon. That could save up to thirty gallons a day per person, or nine million gallons a day.

. . . What about recycling the water? I have heard there are new membrane methods that make it economical. Also we would have less of a disposal problem. Shall I look into this?

Each of these is a concrete suggestion. Once a suggestion is on the table, then it can be developed further and eventually submitted to black hat assessment and yellow hat assessment.

. . . Put on your yellow hats and give me more concrete suggestions. The more we have the better.

. . . John, what suggestion do you have? How could we tackle this problem? Get your yellow hat on.

At this point someone would remark that proposals should come from the 'water experts' and that it was not for amateurs to make such suggestions. It would be the role of the amateurs with their critical thinking to assess the proposals put forward by the experts. This is very much a political idiom. The technicians are there to provide the ideas and the politician is there to assess them. There may indeed be a role for this type of thinking in politics, but it does place the decision makers at the mercy of the experts. In other areas, such as business or personal thinking, the thinker is his or her own expert and must produce the ideas.

Where do the suggestions and the proposals come from? How does the yellow hat thinker come up with a solution?

There is no space in this book to go into the various methods of design and problem solving. I have touched on these subjects in other books of mine. The yellow hat proposals do not need to be special or very clever. They might include routine ways of dealing with such matters. They might include methods that are known to be used elsewhere. They might include putting together some known effects in order to construct a particular solution.

Once the yellow hat has directed the thinker's mind towards coming up with a proposal, the proposal itself may not be hard to find.

. . . Take off your black hat. Instead of assessing the proposals we have so far, put on your yellow hat and give us some more proposals.

. . . Keeping my yellow hat on, I suggest that we let private enterprise sell water at competitive prices.

. . . No, we are not ready to switch into black hat thinking. I do not believe that we have exhausted all possible suggestions. Yes, we do intend to bring in experts and consultants, but let us first establish some possible directions. So it's more yellow hat constructive thinking for the moment.

So yellow hat thinking is concerned with the generation of proposals and also with the positive assessment of the proposals. Between these two aspects there is a third. The third aspect is the developing or 'building up' of a proposal. This is much more than the reactive assessment of a proposal. It is further *construction*. The proposal is modified and improved and strengthened.

Under this improvement aspect of yellow hat thinking comes the correction of faults that have been picked out by black hat thinking. As I made clear, black hat thinking can pick out the faults but has no responsibility for putting them right.

. . . If we hand over the water supply to private enterprise, there is a danger of the town being held to ransom by a monopoly supplier who establishes whatever price he likes.

. . . We could guard against that by putting a ceiling on the price. This would be related to today's pricing with an allowance for inflation.

I want to emphasize that no special cleverness is required by this constructive thinking aspect of the yellow hat. It is just the desire to put forward concrete proposals even if they are very ordinary.

Chapter 26

Yellow Hat Thinking

Speculation

> *Looking into the future.*
> *The value of 'if'.*
> *The best possible scenario.*

Speculation has to do with conjecture and hope. Investors are by their nature speculators even if the word tends to be reserved for builders and currency operators. A speculative builder builds a house without already having a customer. Then he sets out to find a customer.

Any speculator must have a strong sense of potential benefit. There also has to be hope.

Yellow hat thinking is more than just judgement and proposals. It is an attitude that moves ahead of a situation with positive hope. Yellow hat thinking sets out to glimpse possible benefits and values. As soon as there is a glimpse of these, exploration takes place in that direction.

In practice there is a big difference between objective judgement and the intention to find positive value. It is this reaching out and reaching forward aspect of yellow hat thinking that I am indicating with the word *speculation*.

. . . There is a new type of fast food that is becoming popular. It is a sort of flattened chicken cooked in a Mexican style and offered as 'pollo'. Put on your yellow hat and tell me what you see in this.

. . . There are so many different types of insurance that people get confused. Could we have some sort of 'overcoat' insurance that takes everything into account? Take that idea away and give it some yellow hat attention. Come back and tell me what you find.

This speculative aspect of yellow hat thinking is pure *opportunity* thinking. It goes beyond problem solving and improvement. People are forced to solve problems but no one is ever forced to look for opportunities. However, everyone is *free* to look for opportunities – if they so wish.

Speculative thinking must always start off with the best possible scenario. That is the way one can assess the maximum possible benefit from the idea. If the benefits are poor with the best possible scenario, then the idea is not worth pursuing.

. . . In the best possible scenario, the other store is forced out of business and we take over the whole business for the area. But I do not see that this would be especially profitable. As it is, the other store is struggling.

. . . In the best possible scenario, the interest rate rises rapidly and the value of our fixed-rate transferable mortgage makes the house very saleable.

If the benefits seem attractive enough in the best possible scenario, it becomes a matter of seeing how likely that scenario is – and how likely are the benefits to flow as assumed.

In its speculative aspects, yellow hat thinking envisages the best possible scenario and the maximum benefits. Yellow hat thinking can then scale these down in a 'likelihood' manner.

Finally, black hat thinking can indicate the areas of doubt.

Opportunities can arise from the extrapolation into the future of the present scene. Opportunities also arise 'if' some particular event takes place or some condition changes.

. . . Bond prices will rise 'if' interest rates fall.

. . . 'If' fuel prices fall, big cars will become more saleable.

It is part of the speculative function of yellow hat thinking to explore possible 'if' changes.

It is never a matter of basing action or decisions on the basis of an 'if' exploration – although defensive action may need to be taken as with the hedging of funds or the taking out of fire insurance. It is part of yellow hat exploration.

Part of the black hat function was also to explore 'if' in the sense of risk and danger. The corresponding part of the yellow hat function is to explore the positive equivalent of risk, which we call opportunity.

. . . Under what conditions would this hotel chain be profitable?

. . . If satellite broadcasting gets established, what new opportunities is it going to offer to advertisers?

The speculative aspect of yellow hat thinking is also concerned with *vision.*

I mentioned the role of vision and dreams in yellow hat thinking in an earlier section. In a sense vision goes beyond speculation because vision can set a goal which there is little hope of reaching.

In any design there is some sort of vision that comes first. Just as a good salesman makes a sale by putting forth a marvellous vision which the client is invited to share, so the designer sells himself a positive vision of what he is trying to do. The vision comes first and then the form and detail follow. This vision includes both the benefits and the feasibility of the project: it can be done and it is worth doing.

It is very difficult to do anything at all without some sense of achievement and value.

. . . I have this vision of attractive low-cost housing, and I think I can also see how it could be done.

. . . I have this vision of a different type of economics which will handle wealth and productivity in a new way.

. . . I have this vision of thinking being taught as a fundamental subject in every school. It has already started in some countries.

The excitement and stimulation of a vision go far beyond objective judgement. A vision sets direction for thinking and for action. This is a further aspect of yellow hat thinking.

Chapter 27

Yellow Hat Thinking

Relation to Creativity

Difference between constructive and creative.
Effectiveness and change.
New ideas and old ideas.

Yellow hat thinking is not directly concerned with creativity. The creative aspect of thinking is specifically covered by the green thinking hat, which we shall come to next.

It is quite true that the positive aspect of yellow hat thinking is required for creativity. It is true that the positive assessment and constructive aspect of yellow hat thinking is vital to creativity. Nevertheless, yellow hat thinking and green hat thinking are quite distinct.

A person may be an excellent yellow hat thinker and yet be totally uncreative. I see a great danger in confusing the two hats because then a person who is not creative would feel that yellow hat thinking is not for him or her.

Creativity is concerned with change, innovation, invention, new ideas and new alternatives. A person can be an excellent yellow hat thinker and never have a new idea. The effective application of old ideas is a proper exercise of yellow hat thinking. The ideas do not have to be new and there does not even have to be an intention to find new ideas. Yellow hat thinking is concerned with the positive attitude of getting the job done. Effectiveness rather than novelty is what yellow hat thinking is all about.

Some confusion occurs in the English language due to the very broad meaning of the word *creative*. There are two distinct aspects. The first aspect is that of 'bringing something about'. In this sense someone might create a mess. A carpenter creates a chair. An entrepreneur creates a business. The second aspect is that of 'newness'. Again this is confusing because there are two sorts of newness. The first aspect is of something which is new in the sense that it is different from what was there before; for example, a communications system that is 'new' to your office even though it might be in use in thousands of others. The second aspect of 'new' is an absolute newness. That is to say an invention or concept that has not occurred anywhere before.

In regard to artists, there is something of a dilemma. For example, a painter clearly brings into being something that was not there before. Since this painting is unlikely to be exactly the same as a previous painting, there is something 'new'. Yet there may be no new concept or new perception in that painting. The painter may have a strong style and then apply that style to one landscape after another. In a sense there is a production line within a particular style.

Yellow hat thinking is very much concerned with bringing things about. Yellow hat thinking may be concerned with taking an idea that is used elsewhere and putting it to work. Yellow hat thinking may be concerned with generating alternative approaches to a problem. Yellow hat thinking may even define opportunities. But yellow hat thinking is not concerned with changing concepts or perceptions. That is the business of green hat thinking.

Setting out to look at something in a positive way may itself create a new perception and that can occur with yellow hat thinking.

. . . That glass is not half empty but is half full of whisky.

Just as black hat thinking can pinpoint a fault and leave it to green hat thinking to correct the fault, so yellow hat thinking can define an opportunity and leave it to green hat thinking to come up with some novel way of exploiting that opportunity.

. . . More and more people need to park in cities. How can we get some value out of that?

. . . We could raise the room prices if we could attract more business travellers to this hotel. How could we do that? Let us have the usual ideas and then let us put on our green thinking hats in order to find some new ideas.

Chapter 28

Summary of Yellow Hat Thinking

Yellow hat thinking is positive and constructive. The yellow colour symbolizes sunshine, brightness and optimism.

Yellow hat thinking is concerned with positive assessment, just as black hat thinking is concerned with negative assessment.

Yellow hat thinking covers a positive spectrum ranging from the logical and practical at one end to dreams, visions and hopes at the other end.

Yellow hat thinking probes and explores for value and benefit. Yellow hat thinking then strives to find logical support for this value and benefit. Yellow hat thinking seeks to put forward soundly based optimism but is not restricted to this – provided other types of optimism are appropriately labelled.

Yellow hat thinking is constructive and generative. From yellow hat thinking come concrete proposals and suggestions. Yellow hat thinking is concerned with operacy and with making things happen. Effectiveness is the aim of yellow hat constructive thinking.

Yellow hat thinking can be speculative and opportunity seeking. Yellow hat thinking also permits visions and dreams.

Yellow hat thinking is not concerned with mere positive euphoria (red hat) nor directly with creating new ideas (green hat).

THE GREEN HAT

The green hat is the energy hat. Think of vegetation. Think of growth. Think of new leaves and branches. The green hat is the creative hat.

Under the green hat we put forward new ideas. Under the green hat we lay out options and alternatives. These include both the obvious alternatives and fresh ones. Under the green hat we seek to modify and improve suggested ideas.

The value of the green hat is that a specific time is set out for everyone to make a creative effort. Creativity is no longer just the business of the 'idea person' while everyone else sits around waiting to pounce on an idea. When the green hat is in use everyone is expected to make a creative effort – or else keep quiet. People do not like keeping quiet, so they make a creative effort.

The deliberate allocation of time to creative effort is very important. It acknowledges that creativity is a key ingredient in thinking.

The 'expectation' aspect is also very important. People are very good at doing what is expected of them. People are very good at playing the 'game' that they perceive to be in progress. The result is that people who have never thought of themselves as creative start making a creative effort. Their confidence increases and soon they are as creative as anyone else.

Under the green hat you are permitted to put forward 'possibilities'. Possibilities play a much bigger role in thinking than most people believe. Without possibilities you cannot make progress. Two thousand years ago, Chinese technology was way ahead of Western technology. Then progress seemed to come to an end. The explanation often given is that the Chinese did not develop the hypothesis. Without this key piece of mental software it was impossible to make progress.

Those who believe that progress arises from the analysis of information and steps of logical deduction are totally wrong. Without the framework of possibilities we cannot even see the information in new ways.

It is under the green hat that suggested courses of action are put forward: 'We could do this, or this, or this.' The green hat is also used to overcome some of the difficulties put forward under the black hat. The green hat may suggest modifications to an idea to avoid the difficulties. The green hat may suggest the need for an additional idea.

The green hat includes both 'the top of the head' creativity and 'deliberate' creativity.

If the green hat has produced lots of ideas and possibilities, there may not be enough time at that session to consider them all. The red hat may then be used to pick out those ideas that seem to fit a particular frame. For instance, the frame might be 'low-cost ideas' or 'ideas that are easy to test'. The other ideas might be dealt with later. In this way the energy of the green hat may still be used in a practical way.

Chapter 29

The Green Hat

Creative Thinking

New ideas, new concepts and new perceptions.
The deliberate creation of new ideas.
Alternatives and more alternatives.
Change.
New approaches to problems.

The green thinking hat is concerned with new ideas and new ways of looking at things. Green hat thinking is concerned with escaping from the old ideas in order to find better ones. Green hat thinking is concerned with change. Green hat thinking is a deliberate and focused effort in this direction.

. . . Let's have some new ideas on this. Put on your green thinking hats.

. . . We are bogged down. We keep going over the same old ideas. We desperately need a new approach. The time has come for some deliberate green hat thinking. Let's go.

. . . You have laid out the traditional approaches to this problem. We shall come back to them. But first let us have ten minutes of green hat thinking to see if we can come up with a fresh approach.

. . . This demands a green hat solution.

We need creativity because nothing else has worked.

We need creativity because we feel that things could be done in a simpler or better way.

The urge to do things in a better way should be the background to all our thinking. There are times, however, when we need to use creativity in a deliberate and focused manner. The green hat device allows us to switch into the creative role just as the red hat allows us to switch into the 'feeling' role and the black hat into the caution role.

In fact, there may be more need for the green hat than for any other of the thinking hats. In the exercise of creative thinking, it may be necessary to put forward as provocations ideas that are deliberately illogical. We therefore need a way of making it clear to those around that we are deliberately playing the role of jester or clown as we seek to provoke new concepts. Even when they are not provocations, new ideas are delicate seedlings which need the green hat to protect them from the instant frost of black hat habits.

As I have mentioned at various points, the *signalling* value of the six thinking hats has several aspects to it. You can *request* that someone put on a particular hat and then attempt to think in that way. You can *indicate* that a certain type of thinking seems desirable. You can *signal* to others that you are trying to think in a particular manner – and that therefore they should treat your contribution in the appropriate manner. One of the most important aspects is that you can also *signal to yourself*. This is particularly important with the green hat. You deliberately put on the green hat, and this means that you are setting aside time for deliberate creative thinking. This is quite different from simply waiting for ideas to come to you. You may have no new ideas at all while wearing the green hat, but the effort has been made. As you get better at deliberate creative thinking, you will find that the yield of ideas increases. In this way the green hat makes creative thinking a formal part of the thinking process instead of just a luxury.

For most people the idiom of creative thinking is difficult because it is contrary to the natural habits of recognition, judgement and criticism. The brain is designed as a 'recognition machine'. The brain is designed to set up patterns, to use them and to condemn anything that does not 'fit' these patterns. Most thinkers like to be secure. They like to be right. Creativity involves provocation, exploration and risk taking. Creativity involves 'thought experiments'. You cannot tell in advance how the experiment is going to turn out. But you want to be able to carry out the experiment.

. . . Remember, I am wearing the green hat and I am therefore allowed to say things like that. That is what the green hat is for.

. . . I thought we were supposed to be wearing our green hat. We are being much too negative. Isn't that black hat thinking?

. . . My green hat contribution is to suggest that we pay long-stay prisoners a decent pension on their discharge. That could help them get back into society, give them something to lose and prevent them from having to go back to crime. Treat it as a provocation if you like.

. . . Under the protection of the green hat, I want to suggest that we fire the sales force.

The green hat by itself cannot make people more creative. The green hat can, however, give thinkers the time and focus to be more creative. If you spend more time searching for alternatives, you are likely to find more. Very often creative people are only people who spend more time *trying* to be creative because they are more motivated by creativity. The green hat device allows a sort of artificial motivation. It is difficult to motivate someone to be creative, but you can easily request someone to put on his or her green hat and to give a green hat input.

Creativity is more than just being positive and optimistic. Positive and optimistic feelings fit under the red hat. Positive assessment fits under the yellow hat. Green hat thinking demands actual new ideas, new approaches and further alternatives.

With white hat thinking we do expect a definite input of neutral and objective information. With black hat thinking we do expect some specific criticisms. With yellow hat thinking we would like to get positive comments, but this may not always be possible. With red hat thinking we do expect to get a report on the feelings involved even if these are neutral. With green hat thinking, however, we cannot *demand* an input. We can demand an effort. We can demand that time be set aside for generating new ideas. Even so, the thinker may come up with nothing new. What matters is that time has been spent in the effort.

You cannot order yourself (or others) to have a new idea, but you can order yourself (or others) to spend time trying to have a new idea. The green hat provides a formal way of doing this.

Chapter 30

Green Hat Thinking

Lateral Thinking

Lateral thinking and its relation to creativity.
Humour and lateral thinking.
Pattern switching in a self-organizing information system.

In writing about green hat thinking, I have used the word *creativity* because this is the word that is in general use. Many readers of this book will never have heard of me or my concept of lateral thinking. I also want to indicate that green hat thinking covers the broad range of creative endeavour and is not limited to lateral thinking as such.

I invented the term *lateral thinking* in 1967, and it is now officially part of the English language; the *Oxford English Dictionary* records my invention of the term.

The term *lateral thinking* needed to be invented for two reasons. The first reason is the very broad and somewhat vague meaning of the word *creative*, as I indicated under yellow hat thinking. Creativity seems to cover everything from creating confusion to creating a symphony. Lateral thinking is very precisely concerned with changing concepts and perceptions; these are historically determined organizations (patterns) of experience.

The second reason is that lateral thinking is directly based on information behaviour in active self-organizing information systems. Lateral thinking is *pattern switching in an asymmetric patterning system.* I know that sounds very technical, and there is no need to understand the technical basis of lateral thinking in order to use its techniques. The technical basis is there, however, for those who want to know about it. Just as logical thinking is based on the behaviour of symbolic language (a particular universe), so lateral thinking is based on the behaviour of patterning systems (also a particular universe).

As a matter of fact, there is a very close relationship between the mechanisms of humour and the mechanisms of lateral thinking. Both depend on the asymmetric nature of the patterns of perception. This is the basis of the sudden jump or insight after which something becomes obvious.

The deliberate techniques of lateral thinking (various forms of provocation and 'movement') are directly based on the behaviour of patterning systems. The techniques are designed to help the thinker to cut *across* patterns instead of just following along them. When cutting across to a new pattern is seen to make sense, we have the eureka effect.

Much of our thinking culture is directed towards the 'processing' part of thinking. We have developed excellent systems including mathematics, statistics, data processing, language and logic. But all these processing systems can work only on the words, symbols and relationships provided by perception. It is perception which reduces the complex world around us to these forms. It is in perception that lateral thinking works to try to alter the established patterns.

Lateral thinking involves attitudes, idioms, steps and techniques. I have written about these in *Lateral Thinking* and *Lateral Thinking for Management*. This book is not the place to go over them again.

I shall, however, deal with some fundamental points of lateral thinking in the following sections, because these points are also basic to the exercise of green hat thinking.

Chapter 31

Green Hat Thinking

Movement Instead of Judgement

> *Using an idea as a stepping stone.*
> *Where does this take me?*
> *The forward effect of an idea.*

In normal thinking we use *judgement.* How does this idea compare to what I know? How does this idea compare to my established patterns of experience? We judge that it does fit or we point out why it does not fit. Critical thinking and black hat thinking are concerned directly with seeing how well a suggestion fits with what we already know.

We may call this the *backward effect* of an idea. We look backward at our past experience to assess the idea. Just as a description has to fit what it is describing, so we expect ideas to fit our knowledge. How else could we tell if they are correct?

For most of our thinking, judgement (of both yellow and black hat types) is vital. We could not do anything without it. With green hat thinking, however, we have to substitute a different idiom. We replace judgement with *movement.*

Movement is a key idiom of lateral thinking. It is another term that I coined. I want to make it absolutely clear that movement is *not* just an absence of judgement. Many early approaches to creative thinking talk about deferring, suspending or delaying judgement. I think this is much too weak, because it does not actually tell the thinker what to do – only what not to do.

Movement is an active idiom. We use an idea for its *movement value.* There are a number of deliberate ways of getting movement from an idea, including extracting the principle and focusing on the difference.

With movement we use an idea for its *forward effect.* We use an idea to see where it will get us. We use an idea to see what it will lead to. In effect we use an idea to move forward. Just as we use a stepping stone to move across a river from one bank to the other, so we use a provocation as a stepping stone to move across from one pattern to another.

As we shall see, provocation and movement go together. Without the idiom of movement, we cannot use provocation. Unless we are able to use provocation, we remain trapped within past patterns.

. . . I want you to use this idea for its movement value not its judgement value. Suppose everyone became a policeman.

It was just such a provocation that led to the concept of 'neighbourhood watch', which I spelled out in the cover story of *New York Magazine* in April 1971. The concept is now in use in twenty thousand communities in the United States. The idea is that citizens act as extra eyes and ears for the police – in terms of preventing and detecting crime in the neighbourhood. There is said to be a significant fall in crime in areas where the idea is in use.

. . . Suppose we made hamburgers square. What movement could you get out of that idea?

. . . Suppose there were transferable insurance bonds which one person could sell directly to another. Green hat that idea.

This might lead to the idea that insurance was actually transferable. People would then be risk rated themselves. If you were an AAA type risk, you would get certain benefits from the universal insurance bond. If you were only an AA type, you would get lesser benefits.

Sometimes we take an idea and use it as a stepping stone and end up with an idea that is quite different. We merely extract some principle from the stepping stone and then apply that principle. At other times we stay with a 'seedling' idea and nurture it until it grows into a stout plant. It may also be a matter of taking a vague idea and then shaping it into something concrete and practical. All these are aspects of movement. The key thing to remember is that we move *forward* with an idea or from an idea.

. . . Take the suggestion that everyone who wants to be promoted should wear a yellow shirt or blouse. Put on your green hat and tell me where that idea takes you.

. . . It leads me to think of the self-image of the person who has chosen to wear a yellow shirt. He has to live up to that image.

. . . It leads me to think of some way to recognize those people who have ambition but who would not be noticed for their talent. Maybe it would make more sense to train ambitious people and give them the skills.

. . . It leads me to think of the rules of the game. The yellow shirt would be a defined rule of the game of promotion and everyone would know it. How many employees know what they need to do to get promoted?

. . . It leads me to think of those people who do not want to be promoted. They can show this by not wearing the yellow shirt. They just want to stay in their jobs.

. . . It leads me to think of a way of bringing forward the leaders. A person would need to be pretty sure of his standing with those around before he risked putting on the yellow shirt.

From this sort of movement a number of useful ideas could emerge. None of these ideas need actually make use of a yellow shirt as such.

. . . Here is a suggestion for working on Saturdays and having a midweek break on Wednesday. Can you green hat it for me?

. . . As no one wants to work the weekend shifts, there is a suggestion that we employ a permanent Saturday/Sunday workforce, which would be quite separate. It seems an unworkable idea but green hat it.

In fact this last idea was tried out and worked very successfully. Using some green hat thinking on the idea made it seem attractive enough to be tried (in this specific case yellow hat thinking might have done the same).

Movement should go far beyond the positive assessment

of an idea. Movement is a dynamic process, not a judgement process.

What is interesting in this idea? What is different in this idea? What does this idea suggest? What does this idea lead to? Such questions are all part of the movement idiom.

The key point to remember is that in green hat thinking the movement idiom completely replaces the judgement idiom.

Chapter 32
Green Hat Thinking

The Need for Provocation

Use of the word po.
The logic of the absurd.
Random provocation.

Scientific discoveries are always written up as if they had proceeded step by step in a logical fashion. Sometimes this is what indeed did happen. At other times the step-by-step logic is only a hindsight dressing up of what actually happened. An unplanned mistake or accident took place and this provided the provocation that set off the new idea. Antibiotics arose from the accidental contamination of a culture dish with the *Penicillium* mould. It is said that Columbus dared to sail across the Atlantic only because he made a serious error in calculating the distance around the world from an ancient treatise.

Nature provides such provocations. A provocation can never be looked for because it has no place in current thinking. Its role is to jerk thinking out of current patterns.

The logic of provocation arises directly from the logic of asymmetric patterning systems (see *Po: Beyond Yes and No*).

We can sit around and wait for provocations, or we can set out to produce them deliberately. This is what happens in lateral thinking. The ability to use provocations is an essential part of lateral thinking.

In the preceding section we looked at the movement idiom.

That is how we use provocations. We use them for their movement value. We can now look at how we set them up.

Many years ago I invented the word *po* as a symbolic indicator of an idea that was being put forward *as a provocation and for its movement value.* If you like, the letters stand for *provocative operation.*

Po acts as a sort of white flag of truce. If a person approached the castle wall waving a white flag, one would be breaking the rules of the game by shooting that person. Similarly, if an idea is put forward under the protection of po, to shoot it down with black hat judgement would not be playing the game.

In a way – as I mentioned before – the word *po* acts in the same way as the green hat device. A person wearing the green hat is allowed to put forward 'crazy' ideas. The green hat is much broader in scope than po but po is more specific. So it is best to use both.

. . . Po cars should have square wheels.
. . . Po planes should land upside down.
. . . Po shoppers should be paid to buy things.
. . . Po executives should promote themselves.
. . . Po a polluting factory should be downstream of itself.

This last provocation led to the idea of legislating that any factory built alongside a river must have its water input downstream of its own output. In this way the factory would be the first to sample its own pollution.

The word *po* may also be regarded as arising from such words as hy*po*thesis, sup*po*se, *po*ssible and even *po*etry. In all of these, an idea is put out for its forward effect – to provoke something.

By definition an absurd or illogical idea cannot exist within our ordinary experience. Therefore the idea lies outside any existing pattern. In this way a provocation forces us out of habitual patterns of perception. As we move forward from the provocation, three things might happen. We might be unable to make any movement at all. We might drift back to the usual patterns. We might switch to a new pattern.

Just as there are formal methods of getting movement from an idea, so there are formal ways of setting up provocations. These provide the deliberate techniques of lateral thinking.

For example, one simple way of getting a provocation uses *reversal*. You spell out the way something usually happens and then you reverse it or turn it back to front.

. . . Shoppers usually pay for the goods they buy. Let us reverse that. Po, the store pays the customers.

. . . This could lead to the trading stamp idea, which, in effect, paid shoppers a tiny amount for each purchase.

. . . This could lead to the idea that the tills are set up so that at every thousand dollars of input they pay out a jackpot of some sort.

Provocations do not have to be absurd or illogical. It is possible to treat quite serious ideas as provocations. If someone brings you an idea which you do not like and which you can instantly dismiss with your black hat thinking, you can instead put on your green hat and choose to treat that idea *as a provocation*. It is always possible to make this sort of choice.

. . . I do not see how your idea of an 'honour system' store could ever work because it could so easily be abused. But I am going to put on my green hat to treat it as a provocation. That leads to the idea of people adding up their own bills with random checks. Presumably mistakes would even out in each direction.

A very simple way of getting a provocation is to use a random word. You can think of a page number in a dictionary and then open the dictionary at that page. A second number you had thought of could give the position of the word on the page. For example, you might think of page ninety-two, eighth word down. Nouns are easier to use than verbs or other types of words. A list of common nouns is easier to use than a dictionary.

Suppose we wanted some new ideas to do with cigarettes. The random word turns out to be *frog*.

. . . So we have cigarette po frog. A frog suggests hopping, so we could have a cigarette that went out after a short while. This might be of benefit in preventing fires. It could also allow a smoker to have a short smoke and then to use that cigarette later. This in turn leads to a new brand to be called *shorts*, which are indeed designed to be very short and give only a two- to three-minute smoke.

. . . I want some ideas to do with television sets. The random word is cheese, so television po cheese. Cheese has holes, Po the TV screen has holes. What could this mean? Perhaps there could be some 'windows' which would show what was available on selected other channels.

With logic there should be a reason for saying something before it is said. With a provocation there may not be a reason for saying something until *after* it is said. The provocation brings about an effect, and it is the value of this effect which justifies the provocation.

To many people it may seem unthinkable that a random word could be of value in solving a problem. The definition of random means that the word has no special relationship. Yet in the logic of an asymmetric patterning system, it is easy to see why a random word works. It provides a different starting point. As we trace our way back from that new starting point, we increase the chance of arriving back along a track we would never have taken when thinking about the subject directly.

Just as movement is part of the basic idiom of green hat thinking, so too is provocation. When in France you speak French; when wearing the green hat you use provocation and movement as the grammar of creativity.

Chapter 33

Green Hat Thinking

Alternatives

> *Too easily satisfied.*
> *Routes, options and choices.*
> *Levels of alternative.*

In school mathematics you work out a sum and get the answer. You move on to the next sum. There is no point in spending more time on the first sum because if you have the right answer you cannot get a better one.

Many people carry that idiom over into their thinking in later life. As soon as they have an answer to a problem, they stop thinking. They are satisfied with the first answer that comes along. Real life is, however, very different from school sums. There is usually more than one answer. Some answers are much better than others: they cost less, are more reliable or are more easy to implement. There is no reason at all for supposing that the *first* answer has to be the best one. If time is very short and there are a great number of problems to be solved, there might be a reason for being satisfied with the first answer – but not otherwise. Would you like your doctor to settle for the first thing that came into his or her mind and then to stop thinking about your illness?

So we acknowledge the first answer and note that we can always go back to it. Then we set out to look for alternatives. We set out to look for other solutions. When we have a number of alternatives, then we can choose the best by seeing which one fits our needs and our resources.

We may have a perfectly adequate way of doing something, but that does not mean there cannot be a better way. So we set out to find an alternative way. This is the basis of any improvement that is not fault correction or problem solving.

So far in this section I have looked at instances where we already have a way of doing things. Our search for alternatives is really a search for a better way. There are also times when we do not yet have a way of proceeding.

In planning any journey we set out alternative routes. When we have completed the mental map of a situation, we look for alternative routes to our destination.

The notion of alternatives suggests that there is usually more than one way of doing things, more than one way of looking at things.

The acknowledgment that there might be alternatives and the search for these alternatives is a fundamental part of creative thinking. Indeed, the different techniques of lateral thinking are directed to finding new alternatives.

The willingness to look for alternatives (of perception, of explanation, of action) is a key part of green hat thinking.

. . . Our rival newspaper has just raised its price. Put on your green hat and list all our alternatives.

. . . We have received a demand note saying that if we do not pay a large amount of money, our products in the stores will be poisoned. Let's go through the obvious options open to us, then let's put on our green thinking hats to find some further ones.

The search for alternatives implies a creative attitude: the acceptance that there are different approaches. The actual search for alternatives may not require any special creativity until the obvious alternatives have been spelled out. It may simply be a matter of focusing attention on the subject and listing the known ways of dealing with it. This is not sufficient. Just as we need to make an effort to go beyond the first solution, so we should make a creative effort to go beyond the obvious set of alternatives. Strictly speaking we may need only green hat thinking for this extra search. The first part of the search could even come under white hat thinking: 'Go through the approaches that are normally used in such situations.'

In practice it is more convenient to put the whole search for alternatives under green hat thinking.

In business training a great deal of emphasis is put on decision making. Yet the quality of any decision depends very much on the alternatives that are available to the decision maker.

. . . We are going to have to decide on a location for this holiday camp. Put on your green hat and let me have all possible alternatives. Then we can narrow them down.

. . . How are we going to distribute these computers? What are the alternative strategies?

Many people believe that a logical scan will cover all possible alternatives. In a closed system this may be the case, but it is rarely so in real life situations.

. . . There are only three possible alternatives. We can leave the price the same. We can lower it. Or, we can raise it. There is nothing else we can do.

It is true that any possible action on the price must eventually fall into one of these three choices. Yet there are a huge number of possible variations. We can lower the price later. (How much later?) We can lower the price on some of the products. We can change the product and produce a low-price version. We can change our promotion of the product to justify a higher price (leaving the price the same or even raising it). We can lower the price for a while and then raise it again. We could leave the price alone and give special discounts. We could lower the price and then charge extra for options. Once we have considered such options (and there are many, many more), we could indeed classify them under one of the three choices. But listing the three choices does not, itself, generate all these alternatives.

It is a very common fault of rigid thinkers to outline major alternative categories and to go no further.

. . . What I really want to do is both to raise and lower the price at the same time. We shall create a low price commodity line and a high price premium line.

There are different levels of alternative. I have some free time. What shall I do with it? I could go on holiday. I could take a course. I could do a lot of gardening. I could catch up with some work.

If I decide to go on holiday, we move to the next level. What sort of holiday do I want? It could be a sun/sea holiday. It could be a cruise. It could be a sporting holiday. If I decide on a sun/sea holiday, we move to the next level: where do I go? It could be the Mediterranean. It could be the Caribbean. It could be the Pacific Islands. Then there is the matter of choosing how to get there and where to stay.

Whenever we look for an alternative we do so within an accepted framework, which sets the level. Usually we want to stay within that framework.

. . . I asked you for alternative designs for an umbrella handle and you have given me a design for a raincoat.

Occasionally we need to challenge the framework and to move upward to a higher level.

. . . You asked me for alternative ways of loading the trucks. I am going to tell you that it would make more sense to send our product by train.

. . . You asked me to suggest media for the advertising campaign. I am going to tell you that the money would be better spent on public relations.

By all means challenge the framework from time to time and change levels. But also be prepared to generate alternatives within the specified level. Creativity gets a very bad name when creative people always makes a point of solving a different problem from the one they have been given. The dilemma remains a real one: when to work within the given framework and when to break out of it.

We come now to what may be the most difficult point in all of creativity – the creative pause. The creative pause is not there unless we choose to put it there.

Something is going along very smoothly. We have looked for alternatives at the obvious points. We have spelled out different approaches to the problems. What more could we want from creativity?

I once spent several minutes trying hard to turn off an alarm clock that was not ringing. I had not paused to consider that the sound might have been coming from my other alarm clock.

The creative pause arises when we say: 'There is no obvious reason why I should pause at this point to consider alternatives. But I am going to.'

In general we are so problem-oriented that when there are no problems we prefer to move along smoothly rather than to pause to create more thinking work for ourselves.

. . . I don't want to think that we have a problem here because we don't. But I want you to put on your green hat and to have a little creative pause with regard to our normal habit of painting cars before we sell them.

. . . Have a green hat pause on this point: salesmen are paid commission on the sales they make.

. . . Consider the steering wheel of a car. It does its job well. Pause and green hat it.

Chapter 34

Green Hat Thinking

Personality and Skill

Is creativity a matter of skill, talent or personality?
Changing masks is easier than changing faces.
Pride in the exercise of a skill.

I am often asked whether creativity is a matter of skill, talent or personality. The correct answer is that it can be all three. But I do not give that answer. If we make no effort to develop the skill of creativity, it *can only* be a matter of talent and personality. People are much too ready to accept that creativity is a matter of talent or personality, and since they do not have this, they had better leave creativity to others. So I put the emphasis on the deliberate development of creative thinking skill (for example, through lateral thinking techniques). I then point out that some people will still be better at it, just as some people are better at tennis or skiing – but most people can reach a competence level.

I do not like the idea of creativity as a special gift. I prefer to think of it as a normal and necessary part of everyone's thinking. We are not all going to be geniuses, but then every tennis player does not hope to win at Wimbledon.

I am always being told about people who are natural black hat thinkers. They seem to take delight in destroying any idea or suggestion for change. I am asked if it might be possible to soften the personality of such people. I am asked if they could be made more tolerant of creativity even if they never want to use it themselves.

I do not think it is possible to change personality. I do believe that if a person is shown the 'logic' of creativity, there can be a permanent effect on that person's attitude towards creativity. There are several instances in my experience where this has happened. The most practical approach is to use the green hat idiom.

. . . When you are wearing your black thinking hat you do a superb job. I do not want to diminish your critical effectiveness. But what about the green hat? See what you can do with that.

. . . Maybe you prefer to be a one hat thinker. Maybe you are not an all-rounder. Maybe you can sing only one tune. Maybe you will have to remain the negative specialist. We shall bring you into the discussion only when we need black hat thinking.

No one likes to be considered one-sided. A thinker who is superb with the black hat would also like to be considered at least passable with the green hat.

The clear separation of green and black hats means that the black hat expert does not feel that he has to diminish his negativity in order to be creative. When he is being negative he can be as fully negative as before (contrast this with attempts to change personality).

The tragedy mask and the comedy mask are separate. The actor himself does not change. He plays each part to the full depending on which mask he is wearing. Indeed, he takes pride in being able to do both comedy and tragedy. He takes pride in his skill as an actor.

In exactly the same way, a thinker needs to take pride in his or her skill as a thinker. This means an ability to wear each of the six thinking hats and to carry through the appropriate thinking in each case. I did mention this particular point earlier in the book. I am repeating it again here because of this practical problem of dealing with the negative personality.

... At this point we are doing some green hat thinking. If you cannot do that, just keep quiet for the moment.

... You can at least try to use green hat thinking. You will never develop any confidence in it if you do not even try.

Creative thinking is usually in a weak position because it does not seem to be a necessary part of thinking. The formality of the green hat promotes it to being a recognized part of thinking, alongside the other aspects.

Chapter 35

Green Hat Thinking

What Happens to the Ideas?

> *What happens next?*
> *Shaping and tailoring ideas.*
> *The concept manager.*

One of the weakest aspects of creativity is the 'harvesting' of ideas. I have sat in on many creative sessions where a lot of good ideas have emerged. Yet in the report-back stage most of those ideas have not been noticed or picked up by those at the session.

We tend to look only for the final clever solution. We ignore all else. Apart from this clever solution, there may be much else of value. There may be some new concept directions, even though there may be no specific ways of moving in those directions. There may be half-formed ideas which are not yet usable because they need a lot more work. New principles may have emerged even though they are not yet clothed in practical garments. There may have been a shift in 'idea flavour' (the type of idea generated). There may have been a shift in the perceived solution area (where people are looking for solutions). There may be newly defined 'idea-sensitive areas' (areas where a new concept could make a big difference). All these matters should be noted.

It should be part of the creative process to shape and tailor an idea so that it gets closer to filling two sets of needs. The first need is that of the situation. An attempt is made to shape the idea into a usable idea. This is done by bringing in the constraints, which are then used as shapers.

. . . That is a great idea but in its present form it would be much too expensive. Can we shape it so that it is less so?

. . . At the moment the building regulations would not permit us to do that. Can we shape the idea so that it does not contravene the regulations? Is that possible?

. . . That is the right product for a large company. But we are small. Is there any way that we can use the idea?

Note that the constraints are brought in as shapers and not as a rejection screen.

The second set of needs that must be met are those of the people who are going to have to act upon the idea. Sadly, it is not a perfect world. It would be nice if everyone could see in an idea the brilliance and potential that is obvious to the originator of that idea. This is not often the case. Part of the creative process is to shape the idea so that it better fits the need profile of those who are going to have to 'buy' the idea.

. . . At the present moment there is interest only in ideas that save money. Is there any way this idea can be seen as saving money – now or later?

. . . To be acceptable an idea must not be too new. It must be seen to be similar to some old and tried idea that is known to work. What comparisons can we make?

. . . There is a great emphasis on being able to test ideas in a pilot fashion. How could we test this idea?

. . . High tech is the new fashion. Would electronic technology improve this idea?

At times this process may seem to border on the dishonest. Yet there is nothing dishonest in designing a product for the buyer. So ideas need to be designed to fit the needs of the buyer (within the organization).

In some of my writings I have suggested the role of concept manager. This is someone who has the responsibility for stimulating, collecting and shepherding ideas. This is the person who would set up idea-generating sessions. This is the person who would put problems under the noses of those expected to solve them. This is the person who would look after ideas in the same way as a finance manager looks after finance.

If such a person exists, he or she collects the output of the green hat thinking. If not, the output stays with those who have generated it for their own use.

Next is the yellow hat stage. This includes the constructive development of the idea. It also includes the positive assessment and the search for supported benefits and values. Such matters have been discussed under yellow hat thinking.

Black hat thinking comes next. At any stage white hat thinking can be called upon to supply data required for evaluating whether the idea will work or will be valuable even if it does work.

The final stage is red hat thinking: do we like this idea enough to proceed further with it? It may seem strange to subject it to an emotional judgement at the end. It is to be hoped that this emotional judgement is based on the available results of black hat and yellow hat scrutiny. In the end, if there is no enthusiasm for an idea, it is unlikely to succeed, no matter how good it may be.

Chapter 36

Summary of Green Hat Thinking

The green hat is for creative thinking. The person who puts on the green hat is going to use the idioms of creative thinking. Those around are required to treat the output as a creative output. Ideally both thinker and listener should be wearing green hats.

The green colour symbolizes fertility, growth and the value of seeds.

The search for alternatives is a fundamental aspect of green hat thinking. There is a need to go beyond the known and the obvious and the satisfactory.

The green hat thinker uses the creative pause to consider, at any point, whether there might be alternative ideas. There need be no reason for this pause.

In green hat thinking the idiom of movement replaces that of judgement. The thinker seeks to move forward from an idea in order to reach a new idea.

Provocation is an important part of green hat thinking, and is symbolized by the word *po*. A provocation is used to take us out of our usual patterns of thinking. There are many ways of setting up provocations, including the random word method.

Lateral thinking is a set of attitudes, idioms and techniques (including movement, provocation and po) for cutting across patterns in a self-organizing asymmetric patterning system. It is used to generate new concepts and perceptions.

THE BLUE HAT

Think of the blue sky above. Think of 'overview'. The blue hat is for thinking about thinking.

The blue hat is like the conductor of the orchestra. The conductor gets the best out of the orchestra by seeing that what should be done is done at the right time. The blue hat is like the ringmaster of a circus. The blue hat is for the management of thinking. The blue hat is for the organization of thinking. The blue hat is for process control.

Using the blue hat at the beginning of a thinking session defines the situation. The blue hat may seek alternative definitions of a problem. The blue hat lays out the purpose of the thinking. The blue hat lays out what is to be achieved.

It is under the initial blue hat that the agenda or sequence of use of the other hats is laid out. The blue hat may also specify other thinking processes – even if the hats are not to be used. The blue hat sets the thinking 'strategy'. During the session the blue hat keeps the discipline and ensures that people keep to the relevant hat. The blue hat also announces a change of hats.

Typically the blue hat is worn by the facilitator, chairperson or leader of the session. This is a permanent role. In addition, during a specific blue hat session, anyone can make procedural suggestions.

At the end of a session the blue hat asks for the outcome. This may be in the form of a summary, a conclusion, a decision, a solution and so on. The blue hat may even acknowledge that little progress has been made. Under the final blue hat the next steps can be laid out. These might be action steps, or further thinking on some points.

Chapter 37

The Blue Hat

Control of Thinking

> *Thinking about thinking.*
> *Instructions for thinking.*
> *The organization of thinking.*
> *Control of the other hats.*

Wearing the blue hat we are no longer thinking about the subject; instead, we are thinking about the thinking needed to explore that subject. The colour blue symbolizes overview control since the sky covers everything. Blue also suggests detachment and being cool and in control.

Computers follow their programs, which tell them what to do from one moment to the next. The blue hat is the programming hat for human thinking.

Wearing the blue hat we can lay out a plan for thinking with details of what should be happening in a defined sequence. We can also use the blue hat to give moment-to-moment instructions. The different ballet steps need a choreographer to arrange them in sequence. The blue hat is worn when we want to choreograph the steps of our thinking.

This notion of formally structured thinking is very different from the notion of thinking as a free-flowing discussion with no overall structure.

. . . My blue hat thinking definitely suggests that we ought to be looking for alternatives at this point.

. . . We do not have much time to consider this matter, so we must use our time effectively. Would someone like to suggest a blue hat structure for our thinking?

. . . We have not got anywhere so far. Putting on my blue hat I would suggest we have some red hat thinking to clear the air. What do we actually feel about this proposal to decrease overtime?

Thinking often proceeds as drift and waffle and reaction to what turns up from moment to moment. There is a background sense of purpose, but this is never spelled out either as an overall objective or as sub-objectives. Suggestions, judgement, criticism, information and plain emotion are all mixed together in a sort of thinking stew. It seems to be a matter of messing around until a thinker stumbles on some tried approach that seems to achieve what is desired. It is a haphazard exploration of experience strongly guided by negative criticism. The underlying assumption is that reasonably intelligent people provided with enough background information will, in the course of a discussion, list the action options and choose the most suitable.

There is also the assumption that the thinking will be moulded by past experience and present constraints in such a way that an outcome 'evolves' and is purified by criticism. The analogy with evolution is a direct one, for in Darwinian evolution there are survival of the fittest species and in thinking there is the survival of the best-suited idea. For the harsh pressures of the environment, we substitute the harsh pressures of negativity.

In this type of thinking it follows that those taking part already have the proposals from among which the solution is going to be chosen. These proposals may have been arrived at through personal thinking or may have been provided by 'experts'.

In this book I am concerned with the map-making type of thinking in which the terrain is first explored and noted. Then the possible routes are observed and finally a choice of route is made.

Those involved in a situation will claim that their thinking on the matter is taking place all the time and not just when they sit down for a formal discussion. Indeed, the purpose of such discussions is not so much to think as to exchange the results of the thinking that has already taken place beforehand. At this point we are getting close to the argument type of debate which is so typical of Western thinking.

I would be happy if I felt that a great deal of map-making thinking had gone on before the different views were designed. This is only rarely the case. The thinker quickly looks around for a view based on experience and prejudice and then seeks to have that view refined through argument. This is typified by the traditional method of writing essays in school. The pupil is encouraged to write the conclusion in the first line of the essay and then to use the essay to support that conclusion. Thinking is used for support not exploration. The same thing happens with politics and in the courtroom. Both sides start out with established positions.

The to and fro of argument provides the momentum for the thinking. That is why so many people find it easier to think in a group than on their own. Thinking on one's own has much more need of a blue hat structure.

If we are going to adopt the map-making type of thinking, we need to have structure. Attack and defence can no longer provide structure. Just as an explorer needs some plan of procedure, so the thinker needs some organizing structure.

A blue hat structure might provide a plan of what is to happen at every moment – rather like a computer program. More often blue hat thinking controls discussion-type thinking in much the same way as a coachman controls the horses by guiding them from moment to moment.

. . . White hat thinking at this stage.

. . . Now we need some proposals. That means yellow hat thinking. Concrete suggestions please.

. . . Just hold off your black hat thinking for a moment because I am not satisfied with the ideas we have. Let's have some green hat thinking at this point.

Most often it will be a matter of inserting the occasional thinking hat into an ongoing discussion of the traditional type.

. . . I want to get from each of you your red hat thinking on this. If you remember, when you are wearing the red thinking hat you are allowed to put forward your emotions and feelings without having to justify them in any way at all.

. . . You may not know it but you have been using black hat thinking – that is to say negative judgement. You have told us why it will not work. Now I want you to switch for a few moments to yellow hat thinking. This is where you make a positive assessment.

. . . I don't want your opinions or your suggestions. I want a few minutes of pure white hat thinking. The facts and the figures without interpretation.

. . . I think we need to pause and to do some blue hat thinking. Forget about the subject for the moment. How should we organize our thinking?

It should be said that blue hat thinking is not limited to organizing the use of the other hats. Blue hat thinking can also be used to organize other aspects of thinking such as the assessment of priorities or the listing of constraints.

Chapter 38

Blue Hat Thinking

Focus

> *Asking the right questions.*
> *Defining the problem.*
> *Setting the thinking tasks.*

The *focus* aspect is one of the key roles of blue hat thinking. The difference between a good thinker and a poor thinker often lies in the ability to focus. What should the thinking be about? It is not enough to be conscious of the broad purpose of the thinking.

. . . We want to focus on preparing a range of possible responses to price cutting by our competitors.

. . . Let's focus on what each of us wants from this holiday.

. . . Umbrellas and advertising. I want creative ideas on how ordinary umbrellas could be used for advertising.

. . . How can we get satisfied guests to encourage their friends to use our hotel? This is the specific focus.

. . . The broad focus is on finding new market segments to use our fast-food outlets. The tight focus is on getting old people to use our facilities at off-peak times.

A focus can be broad or it can be narrow. Within a broad focus there may be several tight foci. The important thing about a focus is that it should be *spelled out in a definite manner.* Blue hat thinking should be used specifically to bring about definition of the focus. Blue hat thinking should be used to monitor any drift from this focus. Time spent thinking about the thinking is not time wasted.

. . . I am putting on my blue hat to say that we have drifted very far from what we set out to think about. We do have a lot of interesting ideas but none of them are relevant to the starting focus. We need to get back on track. Any more blue hat comments?

. . . Put on your blue hats and say how you think we are doing. Are we getting anywhere?

Asking a question is the simplest way of focusing thinking. It is very often said that asking the right question may be the most important part of thinking. Unfortunately, it is much easier to ask the right questions in hindsight – after the answer has been provided. Nevertheless, careful attention to the framing and focus of a question is an important aspect of blue hat thinking.

Questions are divided into two types. There is a *fishing question*, which is exploratory (like putting bait on a hook but not knowing quite what might turn up). There is a *shooting question*, which is used to check out a point and which has a direct yes or no answer (like aiming at a bird and hitting or missing).

. . . The question is not so much what we do but when we do it. Timing is vital. What factors should we consider in this timing?

. . . The question is whether the tax advantages were really perceived by the client or whether they just provided our salesmen with a convenient selling point for insurance.

A problem is really only a special type of question: how do we achieve this? The definition of the problem is important, otherwise the solution may be irrelevant or unnecessarily cumbersome. Is this the real problem? Why do we want to solve this problem? What is the underlying problem?

. . . The cold weather is not really the problem. People's perception of the cold weather is the problem. That we can change.

. . . The problem is not that we have no snow but that we have no skiing. So we take people in buses to where the snow is.

Instead of presuming to find the best problem definition, it is more practical to set out a range of alternative definitions. This is all part of blue hat thinking.

It is also the role of the blue hat thinker to set specific thinking tasks. This is even more important when an individual is thinking on his or her own.

. . . Set out the objective of this meeting. What sort of outcome would we regard as successful?

. . . Start by listing the areas of agreement between the two parties.

. . . The thinking task is to figure out how we might decide this point here and now.

. . . List four 'idea-sensitive areas' to do with school education.

. . . Black hat our current advertising campaign.

A thinking task may be bite-sized or it may be broad. A thinking task may require a specific achievement or it may ask for input within an area.

. . . I just want some exploratory ideas on this business of shopping via TV.

. . . How can we find out whether their strategy has been successful?

. . . Why are we having difficulty in deciding between these alternatives?

When a thinking task cannot be carried out, then a note of that failure needs to be made.

. . . We have not come up with an explanation of this increase in the eating of sweets. We shall have to come back to it later and see if we can produce some testable hypotheses.

. . . We have not come up with any ideas for increasing the consumption of lamb. Perhaps we had better break it down into sub-problems.

The blue hat thinker holds up the target and says, 'This is it. Shoot in this direction.'

Chapter 39

Blue Hat Thinking

Program Design

> *Step by step.*
> *Software for thinking.*
> *Choreography.*

Computers have their software, which tells them what to do at every instant. Without software a computer cannot work. One of the functions of blue hat thinking is to design software for thinking about a particular matter. It is possible to have fixed structures which can be applied to any situation. What I want to look at in this section is customized software which is designed for each situation.

. . . We will start with some blue hat thinking to design the program we want to follow.

. . . This is an unusual situation. Where do we start? What should we be thinking about?

At the end of the last section I mentioned that most of the time six hat thinking will consist of occasional interventions in the course of normal discussion/argument type thinking. There will be occasional requests for a specific type of thinking symbolized by a thinking hat. Here I want to consider the formal program possibility which does lay down a sequence of steps.

There is free dance in which the dancers improvise from moment to moment in order to express the overall theme. Then there is formal ballet in which each step is precisely determined by the choreography. It is this choreography aspect of blue hat thinking that I am concerned with here. But I do not want the reader to think that this is the way six hat thinking should be used all the time.

I also want to make clear – as I have done before – that blue hat programs can include many more aspects of thinking than just the six hats.

. . . We should start by analysing all the factors that we must take into account in designing this line of children's clothes.

. . . We should start by mapping out the areas of agreement, the areas of disagreement and the areas of irrelevance in this dispute.

The program will vary from situation to situation. The program for solving a problem will differ from the program used to design a boat. A negotiations program will not be the same as a decision program. Even within the area of decision making, the program used for one decision may differ from that used for another. The blue hat thinker customizes the program to fit the situation, just as a carpenter plans how he is going to make a chair or a cabinet.

Should the subject be one about which the thinkers have strong feelings, then it would make sense to put red hat thinking first on the program. This would bring the feelings to the surface and make them visible. Without this red hat thinking each person might seek to express his or her emotions indirectly through other means, such as excessive black hat thinking. Once the emotions are made visible, then a thinker is more free of them. There may even be more pressure on that thinker to be objective.

The next step might be white hat thinking so that all the relevant information can be put on the table. It is usually necessary to go back to white hat thinking from time to time – as a sort of subroutine – in order to check out different points.

Yellow hat thinking is then used to put forward existing proposals and suggestions. There can be an interplay between blue hat thinking and yellow hat thinking as the blue hat thinking asks questions and pinpoints problem areas. White hat thinking can also put forward state-of-the-art approaches to the problem.

. . . In the past what we have done in these situations is as follows.

. . . The traditional approaches are known to you all. Nevertheless, I shall repeat them.

Blue hat thinking might define focus areas that need new concepts. Green hat thinking would then try to generate some new concepts. Alternately, there could be a formal green hat period in which each individual thinker carried out his or her own creative pause.

. . . I would like to see if there might be any simpler ways of adjusting premium payments to an individual's cash flow.

. . . There has to be a better way of selling books. I want to green hat that.

At this point a spell of blue hat thinking would organize the available proposals so that there was a formal list. The proposals might then be put into different categories: those requiring individual appraisal, those requiring further amplification, those which just need to be noted.

A mixture of white hat, yellow hat and green hat thinking might now take place in order to develop and take further each of the proposals. This is the constructive thinking phase.

Pure yellow hat thinking is now used to give a positive assessment to each of the alternatives that are regarded as serious possibilities.

Black hat thinking is now used in a screening sense. The purpose of black hat thinking is to point out which alternatives are impossible or unusable. Black hat thinking can also challenge the value of alternatives that are usable.

Yellow hat and green hat thinking is now used to overcome the objectives made by black hat thinking: faults are to be corrected; weaknesses are to be removed; problems are to be solved.

There is a further black hat scrutiny to point out risks, dangers and shortfalls.

Next might follow a blue hat spell which puts together an overview of what has been achieved and also organizes the 'choice of route' strategy.

Red hat thinking now follows to allow the thinkers to express their feelings on the available choices.

The choice procedure now follows as a mixture of yellow and black hat thinking – looking for the alternative that best fits the needs.

Finally a blue hat session sets out the strategy for thinking about implementation.

All this may seem a rather complex sequence, but in

practice each stage flows naturally into the next one – like changing gears when driving.

Where there is to be a fixed program, it is essential that it be made visible to each person taking part in the thinking. If a thinker knows that a black hat session will be coming up shortly, he or she will feel less compelled to put in black hat interjections for fear that otherwise a point will slip by.

It should be remembered that most thinking is actually a mixture of black and white hats – with unexpressed red hat emotions in the background.

. . . This is what we need to do on this sort of occasion.

. . . This is why what you suggest will not work.

The blue hat program can be predetermined by someone who is leading the thinking session or it can be designed by blue hat thinking on the part of all present at the session.

Chapter 40

Blue Hat Thinking

Summaries and Conclusions

> *Observation and overview.*
> *Comment.*
> *Summaries, conclusions, harvesting and reports.*

The blue hat thinker is looking at the thinking that is taking place. He is the choreographer who designs the steps, but he is also the critic who watches what is happening. The blue hat thinker is not driving the car along the road, but he is watching the driver. He is also noting the route that is being taken.

The blue hat thinker can make comments on what he or she observes.

. . . We are spending too much time arguing about this point. Let us just note it down as a point on which there are conflicting views.

. . . We seem to be much concerned with the cost of this operation, but we have not yet determined if it would provide any benefit. Surely that should come first.

. . . David, you keep pushing this same idea all the time. We do have a note of it as a strong possibility and we will examine it later. I think we should try for some further alternatives. This is meant to be an exploration not an argument.

From time to time the blue hat thinker gives an overview of what has been happening and what has been achieved. He or she is the person who stands by the flip chart and sets out to list the generated alternatives.

. . . Let's summarize what we have achieved so far.

. . . I am going to go through the major points that we have discussed. If someone disagrees with my summary, let me know.

It is the task of the blue hat thinker to pull into shape what may seem to have been a chaotic discussion.

Although I refer to the blue hat thinker as a single person, it is always possible for these blue hat tasks to be carried out by all members of the group. Indeed, one blue hat thinker can ask everyone else to put on the blue hat and carry out the task.

. . . I suggest we pause here. I suggest we all put on our blue hats and spend the next few minutes individually summarizing what we feel has been achieved so far.

. . . Let's go round the table. Put on your blue hats and tell me where we have got to.

Just as it is the role of the blue hat thinker to summarize what has been achieved from time to time, so it is also a blue hat function to pull together the final conclusions.

. . . Wearing my blue hat it seems to me that our conclusions are as follows.

. . . Are we all agreed that these are the conclusions that we reached?

It is the business of blue hat thinking to make the final summary and prepare the report. This does not mean that it is the role of one individual (though it may be). It means that each thinker switches into his blue hat role to comment accurately and objectively on the thinking that has taken place.

One of the blue hat functions is to be a 'photographer' who observes and records the thinking that is taking place and has taken place.

Chapter 41

Blue Hat Thinking

Control and Monitoring

The chairperson.
Discipline and focus.
Who is in charge?

Normally the chairperson at any meeting has an automatic blue hat function. He or she keeps order and makes sure that the agenda is observed.

It is possible to assign a specific blue hat role to someone other than the chairperson. This blue hat thinker will then have the task of monitoring the thinking within the framework set by the chairperson. It may well be that the chairperson is not himself or herself particularly skilled in monitoring thinking.

I also want to emphasize that anyone at a meeting can exercise a blue hat function.

. . . I am reaching for my blue thinking hat to say that Ms Brown's comments are inappropriate at this point.

. . . I am going to put on my blue hat in order to say that I think we are straying away from the central issue.

. . . My blue hat thinking tells me that we should define this point as a key problem, then we should attempt to tackle this problem – now or later.

Blue hat thinking makes sure that the rules of the game are observed. This discipline aspect may be the role of the chairperson or the appointed blue hat thinker, but it is also open to anyone to comment.

. . . This is red hat thinking. We want your feelings, not why you hold them.

. . . I am sorry, that is clearly black hat thinking and out of order at this point.

. . . That is not the way to treat an idea under green hat thinking. You are supposed to use movement not judgement.

. . . Is that really supposed to be white hat information? It seems more like red hat feeling.

. . . The blue hat role is to summarize the thinking that has taken place, not to argue in favour of one alternative.

In practice there is quite a lot of overlap between the different hats and there is no need to be pedantic about it. There may be a lot of overlap between yellow hat and green hat thinking. There may be a lot of overlap between white hat and red hat thinking due to mixtures of facts and opinions.

It is also impractical to keep switching hats with every remark one makes.

What is important is that if a defined thinking mode has been set the thinkers *should be making a conscious effort* to think in that manner. If it is to be yellow hat thinking, then it must be yellow hat thinking.

When no specific hat has been requested, it is unnecessary

to suppose that every single comment must fall under one hat or another. It is also perfectly in order for someone to interject a procedural comment without formally indicating that he is using the blue hat.

On the other hand, it is very important formally to identify the hats from time to time. It is not enough to suppose that the type of hat will follow from the remark. It is precisely the discipline of trying to follow a thinking mode that is important. Otherwise we are back to the waffle and argument mode.

One of the major tasks of blue hat control will be to break up arguments.

. . . I think the increase in turkey meat sales is due to health consciousness.

. . . I think it is simply due to the cheaper price.

At this point a blue hat thinker might ask if there is any white hat information that might settle the point.

. . . As we cannot settle this point, we should note down that there are two offered explanations for this trend. We do not have to decide which is the right one.

So both points are put on the thinking map. In this particular case both points of view may be correct. At other times the two views may be mutually incompatible. Nevertheless, both views can be noted. Further discussion can take place later.

. . . We can now come back to that point we could not decide upon earlier. Would this be seen as predatory pricing? Let us now focus directly upon that point.

. . . Mr Jones thinks that a guarantee on holiday prices will make a big difference to sales. Ms Adams thinks that it will not, and that it could prove very expensive. Let's spend some time examining this point. What does white hat thinking have to offer? If we had had such a guarantee in past years, what would it have cost us?

A powerful way of treating opposing ideas is to suppose that each one is correct *under certain circumstances*.

. . . Under what circumstances would Mr Jones be right? Under what circumstances would Ms Adams be right?

Both sides can then be seen to be right. The next step is to see which of the two sets of circumstances most closely resembles the actual state of affairs.

The same approach can also be used in the evaluation of ideas by using the *best home* method. What would be the best home for this idea?

. . . This product would be wonderful for a large company with market dominance. This other product would be suitable for a small company trying to carve out a market niche. Well, which are we?

There are times when the blue hat thinker has to be quite blunt.

. . . We seem to have got stuck in an argument. We'll note both points of view and come back to it later.

... We are using the map mode and not the argument mode. If you have different points of view, just note them. Don't try to prove that yours is right and the other one is wrong.

... You have both had your say. To go any further is arguing and that is not what we are here to do.

... Will you please stop arguing.

... I want each of you to do some yellow hat thinking on the other person's point of view. That should stop the argument.

The formality of the blue hat allows any thinker to be much more direct than would otherwise be the case.

Chapter 42

Summary of Blue Hat Thinking

The blue hat is the control hat. The blue hat thinker organizes the thinking itself. Blue hat thinking is thinking about the thinking needed to explore the subject.

The blue hat thinker is like the conductor of the orchestra. The blue hat thinker calls for the use of the other hats.

The blue hat thinker defines the subjects towards which the thinking is to be directed. Blue hat thinking sets the focus. Blue hat thinking defines the problems and shapes the questions. Blue hat thinking determines the thinking tasks that are to be carried through.

Blue hat thinking is responsible for summaries, overviews and conclusions. These can take place from time to time in the course of the thinking, and also at the end.

Blue hat thinking monitors the thinking and ensures that the rules of the game are observed. Blue hat thinking stops argument and insists on the map type of thinking. Blue hat thinking enforces the discipline.

Blue hat thinking may be used for occasional interjections which request a hat. Blue hat thinking may also be used to set up a step-by-step sequence of thinking operations which are to be followed just as a dance follows the choreography.

Even when the specific blue hat thinking role is assigned to one person, it is still open to anyone to offer blue hat comments and suggestions.

Chapter 43

Benefits of the Six Hats Method

In practice, one of the most striking things about the use of the Six Hats method is that decisions seem to make themselves. When you come to the final blue hat, the decision is often obvious to everyone present. This seems hard to believe in theory, but happens very often in practice.

The week following a short write-up of the method in the *Financial Times* (London), I had a letter from a man who had been house hunting with his wife. They could not decide whether or not to buy a large house in the country. They had discussed the matter for some hours. The man finally suggested they use the Hats, which he had read about briefly in the newspaper. He wrote to tell me that within ten minutes they had their decision – which satisfied both of them.

To those who have never tried the method it may seem that the hats help you to explore a subject fully and that a specific decision or design stage should follow. This view misses the point that certain hats – the red, yellow and black – are used for assessment, not just information.

If you have to drive to a certain destination and the people involved know the roads only vaguely, there will be a lot of argument about which road to take. If, however, there is a road map laying out the roads, the traffic densities, and the nature of the road surface, then it is easy to choose the best road. The choice has become obvious to all. Exactly the same thing happens with the Six Hats method.

If it is not possible to make a decision, then the final blue hat should lay out why it is not possible. There may be a need for more information at a certain point. There may be different values that cannot be reconciled. So the final blue hat can define a new thinking focus. That new focus can then become the task of a new thinking session.

Special Techniques

Under the final blue hat, it is always possible to bring in special decision-making techniques if these seem required. Such processes are not excluded just because the Six Hats method is in use. But such techniques should be introduced only when it is difficult to reach a conclusion. Most often they will not be necessary and introducing them will just add unnecessary complexity.

Not Surprising

It is not really surprising that with the Six Hats method the decision seems to make itself. After all, when we make decisions on our own, we go through more or less the same process (pros, cons, feelings, facts). The Six Hats method does all that very thoroughly. So what was hitherto carried out in an individual's mind is now done systematically and in the open.

Just as in any other decision-making process, the final decision may be difficult or even impossible to make. It may require balancing two conflicting values. It may depend on speculation about the future – and there is no way of removing the uncertainty about the future. At this point, there is a need to design a way forward that may cover both choices.

If that is not possible and a decision still has to be made, then a red hat decision is made.

In the end, all decisions are really 'red hat'. We lay out the factors but the final decision is emotional.

Conclusion

The biggest enemy of thinking is complexity, for that leads to confusion. When thinking is clear and simple, it becomes more enjoyable and more effective. The Six Thinking Hats concept is very simple to understand. It is also very simple to use.

There are two main purposes to the Six Thinking Hats concept. The first purpose is to simplify thinking by allowing a thinker to deal with one thing at a time. Instead of having to take care of emotions, logic, information, hope and creativity all at the same time, the thinker is able to deal with them separately. Instead of using logic to support a half-disguised emotion, the thinker can bring the emotion to the surface with the red thinking hat without any need to justify it. The black thinking hat can then deal with the logic aspect.

The second main purpose of the Six Thinking Hats concept is to allow a *switch* in thinking. If a person at a meeting has been persistently negative, that person can be asked to take off the black thinking hat. This signals to the person that he or she is being persistently negative. The person may also be asked to put on the yellow thinking hat. That is a direct request to be positive. In this way the six hats provide an idiom that is definite without being offensive. What is most important is that the idiom does not threaten a person's ego or personality. By turning it into role-playing or even a game, the concept of the hats makes it possible to request certain types of thinking. The hats become a sort of shorthand of instruction.

I am not suggesting that at every moment in our thinking we should consciously be using one hat or another. This is quite unnecessary. Occasionally we may want to go through the hats in a formal structured sequence and in such cases we would lay out the structure beforehand. More often we would want to put on one or other hat with some formality in the course of a discussion. Or we may want to request someone else at the discussion to put on a particular hat. At first this may seem a bit awkward but in time it will seem quite natural to make such a request.

It is obvious that the framework will be most useful if all the people in an organization are aware of the rules of the game. For instance all those who are in the habit of meeting to discuss things should become aware of the meaning of the different hats. The concept works best when it has become a sort of common language.

There are many organizations in which the symbolism of the hats has, indeed, become part of everyday language – as a means to direct thinking more effectively.

For information on Dr de Bono's seminars, books and workshops, please contact:

Diane McQuaig
The McQuaig Group
132 Rochester Avenue
Toronto, M4N 1P1 ONT
Canada
Telephone: (416) 488-0008
Fax: (416) 488-4544
E-mail: dmcquaig@debono.com or edwdebono@msn.com

In the UK:
Fax: 44 20 7602 1779

In the United States:
Fax: (515) 278-2245

In Australia:
The de Bono Institute, Melbourne

In Singapore:
TMT Organization

On the Web: www.edwdebono.com